HOW
COPE WITH
SEPARATION
AND DIVORCE

The Daily Express Guides

The Daily Express and Kogan Page have joined forces to publish a series of practical guides offering no-nonsense advice on a wide range of financial, legal and business topics.

Whether you want to manage your money better, make more money, get a new business idea off the ground – and make sure it's legal – there's a Daily Express Guide for you.

Titles published so far include:

Be Your Own Boss!
How to Set Up a Successful Small Business
David Mc Mullan

How to Cut Your Tax Bill Without Breaking the Law
Grant Thornton, Chartered Accountants

Great Ideas for Making Money
Niki Chesworth

Network Marketing
David Barber

You and the Law
A Simple Guide to All Your Legal Problems
Susan Singleton

Your Money
How to Make the Most of it
Niki Chesworth

The Women's Guide to Finance
Ruth Sunderland

Available from all good bookshops, or to obtain further information please contact the publishers at the address below:

Kogan Page Ltd
120 Pentonville Road
London N1 9JN
Tel: 0171-278 0433
Fax: 0171-837 6348

Daily Express

HOW TO COPE WITH SEPARATION AND DIVORCE

DAVID GREEN

KOGAN
PAGE

First published in 1995
Reprinted 1995

Kogan Page Limited
120 Pentonville Road
London N1 9JN

British Library Cataloguing in Publication Data

A CIP record for this book is available from the British Library.

ISBN 0 7494 1544 4

Typeset by Kogan Page
Printed and bound in Great Britain by Clays Ltd, St Ives plc

Contents

Preface

You and your partner face a split.

Maybe that's what you want. Maybe it isn't. But either way all your goal posts are moving. You need to find them again – some very quickly.

Doing that is what this book is about.

Married or not, many of your practical problems will be much the same. You'll have to cope with the same range of feelings and problems with friends, relatives and any children. And the same laws apply to the future residence of, contact with and financial provision for children.

Marriage really only makes these differences:

1. Without divorce you can't marry someone else.
2. Married partners can claim maintenance for themselves on top of any payable for children. The unmarried can't.
3. Married partners may have claims to *any* savings or property which either one has. The rights of the unmarried are far more limited.
4. Before divorce, married people may benefit from their partner's pension. And if their partner dies without making a will they have automatic rights to any of his or her property. Unmarried people do not.
5. Unless remarried or subject to a 'clean break' divorce order, previously married partners may claim financial provision out of the estate of a deceased former partner, however long they have been apart. Unmarried people only have such rights if their partner dies while they are still living together.

Much of the text which follows is therefore likely to be relevant to any couple who part. And it deals separately with the positions of the married and the unmarried where they differ.

Emotional and social problems almost always come first when

relationships fail. Sometimes they last longest. So Chapters 1 to 6 of this book scan a range of personal and emotional difficulties which you and your children may have to face, and offers suggestions for facing them.

Chapters 7 to 9 then look at immediate practical problems – those likely to stare you in the face from the moment you split and how some of them may be tackled.

Finally, Chapters 10 to 19 considers the detail of how and when the law may help – and particularly how you and your partner can yourselves do much to limit its sometimes daunting cost. An understanding of how the legal system works will help you even if you pass everything over to lawyers. But it will help you far more if you and your partner can also use that understanding to solve as many of your own problems as is practical.

David Green
January 1995

Stop press – March 1995

(1) Grounds for Divorce – see pages 78 and 151-152

The Lord Chancellor is to introduce a White Paper to propose reforms to end the quickie divorce. It is likely to echo the proposals of the Law Commission and Green Papers (summarised on pages 151-152). It is not expected to result in changes to the law for some considerable time.

(2) Child Support – see page 88

The Government has introduced a Bill to implement the White Paper 'Improving Child Support'. As anticipated, the Bill mirrors the White Paper. This book covers the White Paper proposals.

(3) Pension Rights – see pages 118, 128 and 134

If enacted, a House of Lords Bill will change the emphasis on pension rights. The courts will have to take them into account and not just have regard to them as before. Pension funds may have to pay part of any pension to a divorced spouse, so that they no longer only benefit directly if their former partner is liable to pay maintenance and the pension forms part of his or her income. If this happens, property transfer and clean break settlements may no longer need to allow for pensions (see pages 128 and 134). As yet there is no proposal actually to split pension funds.

1

While everything is falling apart

Rarely are *both* partners happy to end any relationship. Mostly, one wants a break and the other does not. But both may eventually look back on the period before they parted as one of the most awful in their experience.

'I was caught up in a whirlpool of feelings – shock, disbelief, grief, shame and anger. Divorce happens to other people, not to me. How could something once so beautiful and good now be so dreadful and bad? What have I done to deserve this? What have our children done? How dare this happen?'

Often the partner who wants to break may be just as traumatised.

'Why won't Jo accept it? It's hardly a novelty – look at the figures. Why won't Jo just leave me alone? Why can't Jo face up to it and get on and sort out the details sensibly? How can I be convincing? Why won't Jo just get the message and go away? If only Jo would die....'

Before separation

People may do more damage to each other – and to any children they have – in the period before they separate than they are likely to do to anyone else right through the rest of their lives. Imminent separation may turn both into savages – unrecognisable to friends, relations and even themselves in ordinary life. Violence – verbal and sometimes physical – may erupt even in those to whom it is normally foreign. Others may just close in upon themselves, paralysed by misery, hoping that if they bury their heads in sand it will all go away. Normally reasonable individuals who want a break may turn themselves into monsters, hoping that their very awfulness will convince a partner who does not want a split that he or she would be better off if they did. Those who do not want a break may allow themselves to become desperate, wretched, helpless, clinging caricatures of their usual selves. Both may be scarred afterwards if either falls into any of these traps.

In many cases the actual parting comes as a relief to both partners: 'Blessed numbness with the actual separation – a good condition to be in when dividing things up and experiencing unbelievable spite and pettiness in yourself and your partner as you do it.'

But such relief seldom signifies any final solution. Trauma before separation often becomes deeply ingrained. It can stain the feelings of both partners towards each other, and haunt future relationships for years to come. And if children are involved, they may be haunted in their future – sometimes for the rest of their lives. Avoiding such awfulness may therefore make a profound difference to your whole future – whether you want a break or not.

Should you cut and run?

You're not guaranteed to spare yourself hassle if you just pack your bags and go – out of the blue as far as your partner is concerned. That may be the only practical course in some cases; and if you do that you may in any event start off thinking you have spared yourself the worst.

But instant complete breaks are rarely possible. If there is anything at all which still ties you to your former life – children, family, friends, property or money – you still have to face it, and your former partner, sooner or later. A moonlight flit may create a space in which your former partner can come to terms with the fact that you have gone. But it will also have left him (or her) adrift on an ocean of unanswered questions: Why? Where? How long? What on earth prompted it?

And your partner cannot escape questions children always ask:

'Where's Daddy gone?'
'When will Mummy be coming home?'
'Why doesn't Daddy live with us any more?'
'Mummy can't have loved us. What did we do wrong?'

Managing separation

There are no easy ways out of any crumbling relationship. If people could be entirely honest and totally practical with each other one would tell the other that he or she wanted to end their relationship and the other would say, 'OK, let's sit down and sort out the details.' But such realism is rare even when commercial partnerships fail. It's rarer still when personal ones do. Yet if you want to limit the damage of separation that is still what you should aim for.

Why?

Your starting point has to be a simple if painful reality: once one party to a relationship has decided that he or she wants to end it, there is nothing but misery and injury left for everyone involved until it does end.

Minimising that misery involves facing another reality. Once one of you is hell bent on a break the reasons for what is happening no longer matter. It's not going to make any difference if one of you trots out a list of events he or she has cobbled together to justify what he or she wants, or if the other tries to present a case to persuade them differently. You can't assemble convincing cases to explain or justify how you *feel* – and if you doubt that, remember how friends or relatives may have tried to persuade you that they loved someone, or how you may have tried to persuade them that you did. Nor can you hope to talk someone else out of their feelings with a contrary argument. All that results if either of you try is that each suffers pointless additional hurt.

So the ideal answer is still that you and your partner should sit down together and coolly talk your way through and out of your relationship once either of you says that that's what he or she wants.

Well, that may be the ideal. Of course, the chances are that, if the two of you were able to be that practical with each other on your own, you'd not face separation in the first place. So if crisis does present itself and you cannot be so practical, find yourselves a referee for your debates as soon as you can. Don't leave thoughts of that until you have both already half destroyed each other on your own.

In real life most people need an impartial and skilled referee if they are not to risk lasting damage to all involved when talking their way through relationship crises. And that goes at least as much for those who do not want a break as it does for those who do.

Such referees may be specially equipped for the task – as are many social workers, officers of Relate (listed under Counselling and Advice in Yellow Pages) and family law solicitors who offer mediation.

But the only essential measure of anyone able to help is that they should be able to listen to and comment on what both parties say without criticising either; and, far more difficult, that they should be sufficiently skilled to avoid using words which carry any suggestion of criticism. There is, for example, a world of difference between 'Why didn't you get home before midnight?' and 'What time would you think it reasonable to be home?'

They should also be able to steer any discussion away from arguments about past reasons for you both facing a crisis and towards where you go from here. The past may well have brought you to crisis. But, if it has, reliving it is not going to solve the crisis.

So any referee who is likely to be useful to you must know how and when to say something such as: 'Yes, I understand all your feelings. But they don't change the fact that one of you now wants to end it all. So let us please concentrate on that and on what's to be done for the future.'

Why a referee?

Both of you will behave more like your usual sensible selves in the presence of an outsider – that is human nature. An outsider will also be able to rein both of you in if your feelings run away from the need to look at realities – as they may otherwise do.

Nevertheless, always keep clear in your mind what any form of conciliation is about. No one, you included, can mend a relationship which is already on the rocks. No one can change the feelings of a partner who is convinced that it is on the rocks, even if he or she might later think differently. A referee can mediate between you so that you both may salvage what can be saved from the wreck. However, no one is likely to be able to wave some magic wand between you so as to avoid the wreck altogether – though even that can sometimes result from properly managed mediation.

'All very well,' you may say – particularly if you don't want your relationship to end, 'but what's in it for me? My partner wants it to end and I don't. Why should I make it easy? Why shouldn't I shout, kick, scream and raise merry hell?'

The most obvious answer is that you do not normally shout, kick, scream or raise merry hell – or that if you do you should not be surprised if your partner wants to end it all; and if you nevertheless allow events to drive you into such unusual behaviour, you in the end are the one most likely to suffer.

Think of what those still near and dear to you may say:

'Hell, I never knew Jo was like that. No wonder Les left....'

Think about your own self-respect

'How can I be like this? Why should I let my partner turn me into what I am not?'

Grasp and hold on to the simple if cruel reality that it's over, however bitter, harsh or unjust that may seem. Remember that finding – maybe rediscovering – and then hanging on to your true self, and no longer to a relationship which has now proved unreliable, is the key to your own present and future salvation.

'To thine own self be true' is what matters.

So draw breath before replying any time you feel provoked. Ask yourself if you would normally say what you are about to, or whether your words are only forming as a result of your partner's provocation. Remember that you must now play your own game for your own sake; and that you are not doing it for your partner's.

Who may help?

Divorce Conciliation and Advisory Service, 38 Ebury Street, London SW1W 0LU; 0171 730 2422

Families Need Fathers, 134 Curtain Street, London EC2A 3AR; 0171 613 5060

One Parent Families, 255 Kentish Town Road, London NW5 2LX; 0171 267 1361

Relate (previously Marriage Guidance) – local branches listed under Counselling in *Yellow Pages*. Head office 01788 573241

2

Rediscovering yourself

You have separated

If you are lucky you have managed to part without adding to the grief of most separations. But grief there usually is with any separation which is likely to be permanent, including the ultimate separation when a partner dies.

Of course, death may seem easier to cope with. Death is final. It leaves little practical room for continued questions about how or why. And none at all for where he or she is now, what they are doing, or who they are doing it with. But as far as you and your previous relationship are concerned, the practical results of separation are still best approached as if your former partner has died.

That remains the case even if you keep in touch with his or her ghost. For your partner isn't your partner any more. As a partner he or she *has* died. And the most your partner can now be is a *friendly* ghost. Yet allowing yourselves to become friends is still the single greatest service both of you can now perform for any children you have (see Chapter 5).

What about you?

Your relationship has ended. But you are still shaped by it. Quiet or stormy, every close relationship subtly changes the way we behave, not only with each other but also with everyone else. And the longer the relationship, the greater the change.

Relationships are like tennis matches. Your partner lobs a ball to you, you move and lob it back – or try to. Each move by your partner prompts a move by you, and the same the other way round. Very rapidly you begin to anticipate all of each other's moves. You no longer need to think about how you should respond. Soon your *instincts* govern how you react to each other – and to all around you, children included.

However, once reactions become instinctive they are difficult to root out. So, for example, a man whose wife threw plates at him during his first marriage was still ducking every time a plate-throwing event occurred years after marrying a second wife who never threw anything.

Don't imagine that you will ever easily or quickly get out of your system reactions born during any close relationship.

New adult relationships

Because the patterns of behaviour which evolve in relationships endure long after they end, previous relationships can easily wreck new ones if people enter into them before they have rediscovered themselves. Indeed, this is why so many new relationships, formed during or shortly after previous ones, fail. Quite simply, in such circumstances earlier relationships become part of those which replace them.

How?

Until we wrest ourselves free of previous relationships we all tend instinctively to look first for qualities in new partners which merely fill the most obvious gaps left by old ones. It's as if, unconsciously, we say to ourselves:

'Well, I have (or did have) 1, 3 and 5 from Jo. But I needed 2 and 4 as well to feel right. And it's only now that Les is giving me 2 and 4 that I feel great again.'

But such feelings aren't likely to last. Once Jo has faded into memory, Les's 2 and 4 stand alone. And then there is another yawning gap.

'Oh, hell. I do miss 1, 3 and 5.'

So never underestimate the time it takes to get a former partner out of your system; or the dangers to any future *committed* relationship if you go into one before you have cleared your emotional decks. You must first rediscover yourself if you are not to risk an old relationship dooming a new one. And five years is quite average for the time such rediscovery may take.

But that does not mean that you should lock yourself in a cupboard for five years. Far from it. If you do that you'll be no better off when you come out than you were when you went in. New friendships are part of rediscovering yourself – it's only new *committed* relationships which endanger the process – and which are at risk if it is not completed. And if sex is necessary to you – as it is to most who have once had a sexual relationship – a sexual relationship with a new friend may well also be part of rediscovering yourself. But even new sexual relationships do not also have to become *committed* relationships.

But where then is the boundary between new friendships – with or without sex – and new *committed* relationships? And how do you preserve that boundary?

In most cases the crunch comes with the decision to live together – married or not. As long as you and any new friends have your own homes to go to, each of you is automatically likely to avoid a *committed* relationship. You may visit them and they may visit you. You may sleep together when either of you visits the other. But you can still maintain the essential independence of friendship within that scheme of things.

And that is what matters.

But while you are still rediscovering yourself you and any new friend should also try deliberately to preserve the essential manners of friends – those you would adopt as a visitor in anyone else's house when you visit them; and those which you would offer as host or hostess when anyone else visits you.

So 'Please' and 'Thank you' may continue to matter. If you want something in their house you should not help yourself without first asking. And unless first asked you should not answer their telephone, open their post, or choose their television channel. Indeed, you (and they) may well even continue to phone or otherwise enquire before you call on each other – as friends do.

Quite simply, the process of adjustment is best served if you can keep your own castle; and retain, even if only in form, the right to decide if and to whom its drawbridge shall be lowered; and who and when anyone else shall be admitted.

If you have children such an approach may play a vital part in the chances of them adjusting both to your new circumstances, and to any new friend with whom you may ultimately decide upon a fully committed relationship (see Chapter 5).

Mind you, the end result of any 'uncommitted' approach may be that you and a particular friend finally decide that it offers you both the best long-term relationship. But what's wrong with discovering the best? You already know a good deal about its alternatives.

How to find new friends

Locking yourself indoors will not bring you new friends. Otherwise the ground rules have not changed all that much since you last consciously faced that problem. If you have a job, your job is likely to bring you into contact with new people automatically. If you don't, you will still meet them in shops, pubs, clubs, parks, libraries and associations. There's also a growing number of societies set up just for people in the same boat as you. But you may discover that there is sometimes a touch of desperation which you do not want in groups so single-mindedly seeking to fill gaps in their lives. Finally, you may even risk computer dating or lonely hearts columns in newspapers, but money you can ill afford to spend is likely to be spent far more profitably if you use it merely to put yourself back into general circulation.

Your only real problem may be that this time round you have to do it on your own. The gang or particular friends you used to go around with may well all be tied up with their own relationships now and you may suddenly sense yourself unwelcome in their company (see Chapter 3).

But do you need a team?

After all, what you are now is independent. And that's not the same as being alone unless you let it be.

What about your image?

No one can put the clock back.

You have to rediscover yourself as you are – or should be – now, not try to get back to where you think you were when your previous relationship started.

You may well decide that this is the time to lose some weight, or to put some on, or generally to get yourself fit again. And there's certainly no harm in that. People tend to go to pieces physically under the stress of failing relationships and repairing damage of that nature is good for morale.

Think hard about adding new ornaments to your image. You may have had (or wanted) short or long hair, or a sports car, or an open-necked shirt with a dangling medal. You may have worn mini skirts or long ones, or high or low heels when your previous relationship began. For that matter, you may well fancy what people of the age you then were are wearing or doing now. But unless you want to risk looking ridiculous, first have a good, close look at current styles and fashions and people of and around your own age before you lunge for any replay of where you think you once were, or now ought to be.

Within the self-contained semi-isolation of committed relationships most of us tend to drift away from general fashionable circulation over a period of time. But if as a result you now feel a bit like Rip van Winkle, newly reawakened in ordinary social life, try not to react without thought to its challenges. The disguises which seemed normal when you went to sleep may not be quite so normal now.

Who may help?

See *Yellow Pages:*
National Helplines listed on front pages.
Local support and contact groups listed under:
Clubs and Associations
Social Service and Welfare Organisations

3

Friends and relations

You, your family and friends

Friends and relations instinctively take sides when relationships crumble – with partners to whom they are related, or with whom they are particularly friendly. And in the short term such support may be helpful.

But beware the long-term results of deliberately seeking sympathy.

Few of us are our normal selves when close relationships crumble. And in such abnormal states many of us feel a particular need to justify ourselves, condemn our partners, or both. Even if we then stick to facts and avoid embroidering them, we still tend to highlight facts which favour us, and disfavour our partners. And merely by doing that we may paint false pictures which, sooner or later, catch up with us again.

Take Anne's case, for example. Anne was a capable woman. She was also ambitious and determined to show that she could do anything. Her husband was far more easy going. But, recognising her urge to shine, he was content to go on quietly putting all life's basics in place, and leave Anne to claim all the credit. He made the cakes. But she iced them and claimed all the applause.

The trouble was that over time Anne began to believe her own propaganda. She was doing everything. He was doing nothing. She was carrying all the burdens. He was useless. And that's how she began to describe her life to her family and friends.

Her list of his failings lengthened once she started having the odd casual affair. With so useless a husband she reckoned that she was entitled to a bit of fun; and anyway, she was far too clever to get caught. She then needed an even more convincing list of his faults –

if only to justify what she was doing to herself. She made sure that her family and friends knew all of them just in case things did blow up. Of course, she did not also tell them about the affairs.

But then she did get caught. As so many do she fell in love with one of her lovers.

The fat was really in the fire. Anne and her husband parted. But to the surprise of many their children stayed with him.

At first all her family and friends rallied round her. They were as sympathetic as anyone could be, though she had to be even more inventive to explain the children's decision.

'Well, it's no surprise to us,' they said. 'We can't understand why you didn't leave him years ago. You've had a dreadful time. You've got your own life to lead. But he's useless. How on earth is he going to manage with the children as well...?"

Given the picture she had painted, they were nearly as hostile to her husband when they saw him as they were supportive of her. They had already begun to realise that if they were still to see the children they might have to try to hide some of their feelings. But they didn't expect that problem to last. After all, the husband was so useless that the children would soon be back with Anne – where, of course, they should be.

However, that was not how it worked out. Anne's husband turned out to be perfectly able to manage. Indeed, he was soon coping successfully with everything Anne used to do and everything he used to do as well. And he'd always kept his problems to himself so his family and friends had no surprises.

But Anne's did. With the way things had turned out her husband could not be as she had painted him. And if she hadn't actually lied she must certainly have been selective with the truth. Her friends and family began to drift away from her. Her husband kept his.

Stories such as this recur over and over. Change the sex of the partners and many women who have quietly survived such relationships will recognise the pattern. But the message of Anne's story is clear. If you want to keep the love and support of your friends and family (and for that matter of your partner while you are still living together), don't swamp them with news of your partner's failings. If you do you'll look stupid for having stayed with your partner while you were still together. And after separation subsequent events may convince them, and any children you have, that the fault was all yours – which is unlikely.

Anne's story also has a moral for friends and relations.

Listen, of course, but never judge. Don't ever take all you hear as gospel. And don't take sides. While people are living together their problems are for them to sort out. Any practical help which can be offered to either should never be refused after they split. But other problems are still for them to resolve.

Blood is thicker than water. As long as you have not too obviously deceived them, your family is always likely to remain closer to, and more supportive of, you.

Your friends are a different matter.

All through life, like seeks like. While you and your partner were a couple you made friends with other couples. But their doors are closing now you have separated. The invitations are drying up. Everyone seems to be busy with something else when you call. Why?

No one puts up any signs. However, you have become a silent menace in coupledom and are no longer welcome. Partners of your own sex no longer invite you for fear you and *their* partner may end up fancying each other. Partners of the opposite sex no longer invite you for fear *their* partner may read an invitation as a sign that you fancy each other. And couples whose own relationships may be a bit shaky – as so many are – may well be bonded in an identical fear; your new independence and freedom might look attractive and give the other one ideas.

Couples who still continue to invite you, despite such inner anxieties, may nevertheless insure themselves against the fears that you prompt. A standard manoeuvre is to provide you with a blind date – all too often someone wholly unacceptable.

People often work their way round to that solution by first agreeing, when they discuss your plight, that your new life must be terribly sad and lonely. They might, of course, face difficult questions about their own lives if they expressed a different view. But at least that approach gives them a safe platform from which they can make plans for you:

'Jo's so alone now. We can't leave Jo out. I know, let's invite Les as well. They're in the same boat and they are quite like each other. They ought to get on.'

For formal occasions such couples may merely resort to crude geometry to calm their unspoken unease:

'The table won't look right if we seat two men (or women) together. We've got to invite Jo. So let's ask Les as well. Then we can put the two of them together.'

If your former friends include heterosexual and gay couples such unspoken influences may be all the more obvious. You may be off the invitation lists. But heterosexual couples somehow still manage to fit gay couples into seating plans; and gays don't seem to face any problem with heterosexuals.

What can you do about it?

Probably very little with couples. Their real dilemma lies in their secret thoughts. But spelling them out is not likely to change them.

'OK. So that may be what it's really about...but it might still happen....'

So most of the answer lies with new friends. And most of that with new friends who are already in the same boat as you, and know exactly what it's all about.

Don't despair. There are plenty of them. Well over half of the 26 million households in Great Britain now have only one adult in them. With four out of every ten marriages breaking up, and goodness knows how many unmarried couples as well, you are not exactly alone. And within this multitude of new singles you are more than likely to find the sort of friendship and support you need, upon which people used to rely in their own natural extended families before modern mobile living blew us all apart.

4

Your former partner

Your own future may be a lot easier if your former partner just disappears out of your life. If that is reasonable and possible you can both get over whatever grief either of you feel much as you would if the other had died.

But it may not be possible if work or any other part of ordinary life still brings you together. And your partner's disappearance will not make your life any easier if you have children.

You, your partner and your children

One of you may have fallen out of love with the other. Both of you may have fallen out of love with each other. But your children are never likely to fall out of *their* love for either of you. And there are not many parents who ever fall out of love with their children.

In the vast majority of cases children will still want and need the freest possible continued contact with *both* parents; parents no longer able to live with their children will want and may also need to continue that contact; and any parent who breaks or tries to prevent that contact may be guilty of what is, for children, the ultimate cruelty of which parents are capable after separation (see Chapter 5).

However, any contact between your former partner and your children almost inevitably also involves continued contact with you.

How to cope with continued contact

It's never easy for anyone to resist the temptation to go over old ground (or sometimes to debate new problems) when circumstances bring former partners together again. But that is what you must aim to resist – for your own sake never mind that of your children. Launching into further argument is much the same as deliberately reopening a slowly healing wound. It delays still further the time when you are likely to recover your full and complete independence. And if your former partner begins to argue old scores, reacting merely draws you back into any chaos which accompanied the ending of your relationship – which also erodes progress towards necessary independence. Indeed, you lapse back into being as much your former partner's creature as your own if you enter, or allow yourself to be drawn into further argument.

Yet there are often things which former partners do still have to *discuss*. And if you have children that is likely to remain the case until they are all grown up, and maybe even after that. So it may still be necessary for one of you to invite *discussion*, and for the other to join in. And more often than not there won't be any handy referee when such occasions arise.

You have to draw lines in such circumstances. The essential line is between *discussion* and *argument*. The basic ground rules in the next section may help to define that line a little more precisely.

Don'ts in any necessary discussion

1. Don't get involved in debates – either way – about events before you separated. Who did what; or why or when or how they did it while you were together may still gnaw away at you. But any answers you manage to squeeze out are not going to make much difference to where you are now.
2. Don't argue about anything which has already been settled in court; or by legal agreements; or by any similar legal process.

    You may face all sorts of misery and hardship because of court (or Child Support Agency) decisions about money or property; or about your contact with or the residence of your children. You may well feel that all the misery or hardship is the fault of your former partner, if only because your former partner was on the other side. But neither of you had (or has) any privileged position in such matters. Nor, though people still seem to have a magical belief in the abilities of good lawyers, do lawyers or other representatives make much difference to the legal end results in family matters. Courts and other agencies have long been under a duty to concentrate independently on facts and realities in financial matters, and on how they see the best interests of children in anything that affects them. Former partners (and sometimes children) are entitled to put facts before courts and other agencies. But it is the court or agency which makes the decision: and it bases the decision on principles laid down by law, not on what anyone may say.

So keep clear in your mind that if a decision is anyone's *fault*, it is the fault of the court or agency which made it and not your partner. If you don't like a decision your only effective course is to go back to the court or agency and see if it will change it. Don't therefore meet your former partner with demands for more than a court has allowed, or that he or she agree less.

But don't ever be afraid to be generous and to *offer* more if you wish.

3. Don't burden your former partner with your new problems – former partners have enough of their own. If your former partner asks how you are getting on, of course, there's no harm in answering, as you might anyone. But don't take it for granted that your former partner is still as interested in your problems as he or she may have been while you were together. Far too many people seem to imagine that they are still entitled to bend a former partner's ear to new difficulties. And curiously, people who wanted to get out of relationships seem particularly likely to do that. It's pointless in such circumstances. No one is likely to convince any former partner that a life they chose deserves sympathy.

4. If you have to discuss an issue, don't allow yourself to drift into making (or answering) demands about it. Talking round a subject, discovering what both of you would like to happen, and reaching agreement as a result is one thing, but any chance of discussion and agreement dies the moment either of you starts to make *demands*. Only *rights* justify demands. Any debate which reduces to a question of rights can only be solved by law and lawyers. You have to leave rights and demands to them if that's where you end up. You don't keep a dog and then bark yourself.

Discussions with children around

The don'ts considered in the previous section matter most if your children are in earshot when you and your former partner talk, and always remember that children have very keen ears.

Your children's basic sense of security now rests with the parent with whom they live. But they still need to feel sure that *both* of you can cope with the new lives you are leading; and that there are no problems in your separate lives which imperil their position with either of you, or their future relationships with both of you. They cannot preserve or acquire that sense of security if they know that you and your former partner are still at each others' throats.

Discussions about children

Even when parents live happily together children spot negotiating chances as quickly as anyone. If they once discover that when one of you says 'No' the other may still say 'Yes', they are likely to try playing each of you off against the other for the rest of your lives. And that normal basic skill will quickly refine into real cunning if you and your partner separate.

Yet both of you will suffer in the end if you ever allow your children to play both ends against the middle. Soft or hard touch, their respect for both of you will shrink. They will be in charge of you, not you of them. And they won't be slow to realise it.

So reaching agreement, beforehand and in private, on anything which affects your children also plays a vital part in preserving the stable and predictable relationship which all children need with both parents.

With that in mind, here are some final don'ts and dos:

1. Don't use your children to lever concessions out of your former partner, especially if they know what you are doing. If your children want bicycles, for example, don't:

    (a) tell them you can't afford them and that they'll have to ask your partner;

    (b) tell them that your partner will buy them – unless that has already been privately agreed between you;

(c) greet your partner with the news that he or she is to buy bicycles when your partner arrives to visit the children.

2. Don't give your children special treats or gifts without first discussing and agreeing privately with your former partner that they should be given.

3. If you do agree to make a special treat or gift to your children, try to agree also to present it as a gift from you both, without distinction as to who paid or contributed what. You may want to earn Brownie points yourself, particularly if you no longer live with your children. But there is no going back for either of you once you set off down that road. If either of you is discovered in the mantle of Father Christmas, it won't be long before your children always reckon it worthwhile to bid for or against you – and to withhold their favours if you fail to stump up.

5

Your children

Children notice

'Don't worry. Children soon forget.' That used to be accepted lore. It's a lie.

Children do not forget. When we crumble into old age childhood memories endure after all others fade. The only real difference between children and adults is that children still have to discover how to put things into perspective; and how to tell others – particularly parents – about their feelings.

As a result, childhood experiences can be far more frightening than an adult would find them, simply because a child does not have enough experience of life to allow him or her to put it on to any sort of scale. Moreover, because children do not have words sufficient to allow them to let anxieties out, they tend to lock those anxieties away inside themselves and freeze them unsolved. But those anxieties are still there. And children are still haunted by them.

It follows that there is never any ideal time for parents to separate. Some distress is likely even if parents part when children are fully grown and independent, though adults usually cope.

Nevertheless, children's emotional need of parents and their vulnerability to parental separation do change with age. So it is important that any couple who face separation should remind themselves (and then remember) how relationships with their children would probably have evolved had they stayed together. And parents who love their children will do all they can to allow that process to continue after separation.

How children learn from parents

Most of the way we behave as adults comes from our parents. We end up doing as they did if we found their ways acceptable; and doing something different, often the opposite, if we did not. Most of what we see as our proper adult role with members of the opposite sex also comes from our parents – again either through copying, or refusing to copy. However, the way we learn changes as we grow. And the importance to us of mothers and fathers in the learning process changes as we grow and differs depending on our own sex.

We usually view our parents as perfect in the earliest years of our lives, and after that only slowly become more critical up to the age of puberty. But even in that period one parent is likely to be more perfect than the other. Until adolescence boys tend to be far closer to (and so have a greater need for) their mothers and girls their fathers. We seldom realise it but it is in that period of our lives that we learn most about the other sex – until we begin to add our own direct experience.

With early puberty comes a sea change.

Boys' first allegiance – and need – transfers to their fathers and girls' to their mothers. That is when we begin to learn more about our own sex. But we also then become more critical of both parents. We know more about what we want, and are learning ever more about what other people and other families have and do. Our family and parents no longer shape up so well when faced with comparisons and competition. Increasingly we say so.

Unless our parents have proved remarkably good at bringing us up we become ever more critical as adolescence progresses. We are no longer willing to be told. We know better. We begin to detach ourselves from both parents. As far as we are concerned they have taught us all they can. The world's not the same as it was when they were our age. We now want to find out for ourselves. We know what the law allows people of 16, 17 and 18 to do. We want the independence to do it. Parental stock may fall to its lowest levels in this period.

Finally, we end up with our longed-for independence. Then we begin to discover what we can, in fact, do with it. If our parents have got it right that produces our final reassessment. We end up with an adult, balanced and mature view of them. No longer are they the god-like angels we thought them to be in the first years of our lives. Nor are they the stupid, uncomprehending devils we may have imagined them to be in late adolescence. If we remain particularly close to one in preference to the other, that closeness is now founded on what we actually know of them, not on what we needed to know. They really are quite ordinary people after all. Not so bad. They'll do.

Mostly that is how it happens in families which manage to stay together. But it is important to spell it out. If parents separate and their children are still to tread the same road to maturity – in themselves and in their relationships with others – parents must deliberately design the way they are all going to relate to each other. That is what generous continued contact with both parents is all about.

Maintaining contact

As parents, you may or may not want continued contact. But as parents caring for your children you face the reality that they still need to end up with a balanced view of both of you; and the only way they can do that is through continued contact.

There is more to this than merely making sure that children can still keep in touch. Contact alone may be of limited value if you cannot also bury any hatchets you may still be tempted to wield against each other. Apart from obvious rows in front of your children, you should both try to avoid any temptation to score points against each other with your children – and that includes trying to buy their favour with gifts (see Chapter 4, pages 29–30). Your children will have their own views of you both anyway, and you must try to leave it to them to sort those views out. If either of you sets out to win their support against the other they may seem to take your side, particularly if they are young. But if they feel forced to take a side in which they do not believe, they will eventually have little but contempt for the parent who forces that position on them.

You should both also concentrate hard on rebuilding your children's sense of security with the two of you. The predictability and certainty of what parents do lies at the bedrock of children's sense of security.

1. If your children live with you, try to avoid anything which is likely to get in the way of arrangements made for them to see their other parent.
2. If you live apart from your children, try to be scrupulous in sticking precisely to every arrangement you make to see them or do things for or with them.
3. Remember that as your children get older they may choose to do other things away from both of you – whatever arrangements you have made; and that it is normal for children to do such things, and a sign of their confidence in you if they feel free to.

Finally, some basic matters.

You may at first find it difficult to tell others that your relationship has collapsed. Your children will find it even more difficult. So make sure that you do the telling wherever it may affect them. Tell the head teacher of their school at once. The school will then keep an extra eye on them and be extra sympathetic if problems arise. Schools will also then be on their guard in case anyone collects the children from school who should not do so, including your former partner if things are really difficult between you. And if your children go to clubs or other organisations, have a quiet word with whoever is in charge – for the same reasons.

What might happen if you get it wrong

Details from real life make it easier to understand what can happen if you get it wrong:

Ellen was three when her parents split up. Her mother told her that her father was a drunkard and a wastrel and did everything she could – entirely successfully – to prevent any future contact between them. But Ellen did not know about drunkards and wastrels. She had lost a perfect father. And as her mother said he was no good, that was her mother's fault.

Then Ellen's mother remarried. That made things worse. The second father in real life hadn't a hope of matching Ellen's fantasy memory of a perfect father. As she grew older she became more difficult – as far as her mother and stepfather were concerned – because she was ever more resentful of them and of everything they did.

Finally, Ellen went looking for her real father. She was 18 when she found him. He turned out to be quite ordinary – neither the monster her mother had painted nor the hero Ellen had imagined. And had Ellen had contact with him over all the years since her parents split up, she would by then have been able to see that. She would have had a balanced view of both her parents, and of her stepfather as well. But, as it was, her image of her father was stuck in the groove carved in her memory at the age of three. And there was no way in real life that her mother and stepfather could ever equal it.

Ellen went back to her mother's house. She packed her bags, told her mother and stepfather that she was going to live with her real father, and that she wasn't going to have any more to do with them. And she did just that. But as a result she was not able even to begin to tackle a vital part of her growing up until she was 18. And her mother and stepfather had to write off everything they had tried to do while she did it.

Margaret's background was much like Ellen's. But Margaret had already had a traumatic marriage and was a good deal older than Ellen when she finally found her real father. By then he had long since remarried and had adult children by his second marriage. And he could not cope with the sudden arrival of a middle-aged daughter who felt a desperate need for the sort of love she felt she should have had from him since she was a young child. Faced with what seemed to her like a final betrayal Margaret haunted her father and his new family for years after, as she tried in vain to be admitted to his love.

Ann and John were six and three when their parents split up. The parents' parting was bitter and resentful. From then on their mother took the view that their father's job was simply to pay – in cash; by being furiously reminded of real and imagined sins every time he turned up to see the children; and by having his every contact with them hedged around with demands and restrictions. Both children grew up in an environment in which any sign of favour to their father was treated as disloyalty by their mother.

At first Ann missed and clung to her father more than John

did. They were of that age. But with the onset of puberty she turned more to her mother, as girls do, and then adopted many of her mother's attitudes to her father and to everything else. But she did at least have her mother.

John was not even that lucky. By the time he reached puberty it was seldom possible for his father to see him – his mother had by then moved them several hundred miles apart – and his mother continued to make things difficult when his father did come. As a result John's image of his father remained that of a remote and idealised visitor; and when his mother remarried, his new stepfather had no hope of providing any substitute.

In the end John polarised as much in his father's favour as his sister did in his mother's and he also suffered a serious breakdown.

It was only after Ann and John grew up and left home that they began to feel free to visit their father as they wished. Thus they were both well on into adult life before they had any chance of beginning to build a more balanced view of their parents. But the disorder in their upbringing left them with permanent problems in their relationships with others.

Mary and Joan were eight and nine when their parents split up. On the face of it their parents had reasons which were at least as convincing as those in the other cases for not wanting to have any more to do with each other. But they managed to put those reasons behind them. Mary and Joan continued to live with their mother, and their father continued to maintain them, as frequently happens. But their mother did everything she could to make it easy for them to see and be with their father as often and as flexibly as possible. And their father did everything he could to maintain that regular contact.

As a result both girls grew up with a clear and balanced view of their parents and faced no deep-rooted problems in their relationships with others. And they even coped philosophically with the most challenging problem which faces children and parents in all broken families – what do you do if mother or father finds a new partner?

The next chapter looks at that problem.

6

Children and step-parents

Basics

The relationship between children, parents and step-parents is the most difficult of all human relationships.

Even while still living together natural parents may find themselves at odds once they have children. We are reared to believe in exclusive, one-to-one love and care in our adult relationships. Children immediately introduce competition for that love and care. And even the fact that competition from one's own children is accepted as natural may not prevent friction – though it will seldom have the dire results likely if parents find new adult lovers.

But there is no similar natural instinct to protect step relationships. Stepchildren automatically present themselves to step-parents as competitors for the affection of their natural parent. And step-parents almost always so present themselves to stepchildren.

This instinctive competition is so universal that people have recognised its end results for centuries – it's why wicked stepfathers and stepmothers feature so often in fairy tales. It's also why step-parents feature so regularly in reported child abuse cases. Of course, such extreme problems only emerge in a tiny handful of families in which new relationships have got completely out of hand, but no one should imagine that any triangle involving children, parents and step-parents is ever easy.

All of us need to understand why. Only with understanding are we likely to find it easier to cope.

Separation strengthens awareness of child–parent bonds

By natural instinct children attach to and care for their parents; and parents attach to and care for their children. Without that instinct the human race would never have prospered. But that instinct does not vanish if parents separate – most children and parents become more acutely aware of it. Separation threatens the chances of mutual love and care. Children and parents cling to each other all the harder as a result.

Enter the step-parent

What happens if a parent acquires a new partner? Separation has already sharpened parent–child and child–parent emotional ties. Any new partner threatens those ties in everyway. The new partner competes directly with the children for the affection of the parent who has found that partner. He or she also threatens the children's relationship with their other parent. Children sense at once that a new partner is poised to replace that parent. And that anxiety may become a certain fear if anyone is foolish enough to describe a new partner as a new parent. 'Call me Daddy (or Mummy)' is lethal language between step-parent and stepchild.

Even adult children are likely to share such anxieties. The younger children are, the more they will both feel and suffer from them. And children are far more likely to react to fear than adults – and often violently.

How children may react

Children may become openly contemptuous of a step-parent. They may challenge anything he or she says or does. They may become increasingly more quarrelsome to attract attention, even become violent or start smashing things up.

In the presence of a new partner children may attach themselves more aggressively to their natural parent. If they see the two adults close together or having a cuddle they will often try to squeeze between them. They may go to great lengths to position themselves between parent and step-parent on other occasions – at table, for example. And children are quite capable of setting out to provoke anger in a step-parent just to see whose side their natural parent is on. When it comes to testing out adults, children may be as devious and subtle as any adult – and far more violent in what they say and do.

How adults may respond

Many parents and step-parents judge such behaviour far too simply – as if it's merely a matter of children behaving badly, sometimes very badly.

If that's the way they see it, natural parents may then simply shout at or punish their children. But that is likely to make children's sense of rejection worse. And if it does, their behaviour will become even worse.

If provoked, even saintly step-parents are also likely to lose their rag in the end. That may be exactly what the children want. If children want to show that they reject a step-parent, an angry reaction will tell them that they are succeeding – and they are then likely to try even harder. And if they want to test out whose side their natural parent is on, what better than provoking a row with their step-parent?

If there is such a row, what can the natural parent do? Support the children and risk his or her relationship with the step-parent? Support the step-parent and risk his or her relationship with the children? Or tell the children and the step-parent that they must sort it out between them, and risk increasing contempt from both sides for being spineless and ineffective?

If things get to that stage, no one can win.

Half-brothers and sisters

Half-brothers and half-sisters raise a whole new set of dangers even if parents and step-parents think that they have overcome their problems with existing children. You and your new partner may, with extra love and care, calm your children's anxieties about your own relationship. But you are never likely to rub them out altogether. And if you decide to have a child of your own, all the old fears may flare up again and you will have to put in a lot of loving overtime to calm them.

What your children most fear is rejection by you and exclusion from you. And as far as they are concerned any child by you and your new partner looks likely to drive a final wedge between you.

There is sometimes reason for such fears. Existing children often create a sense of insecurity between parents and step-parents. And when that is so adults can easily see freezing out those stepchildren as an answer. Parents and step-parents may well want a child of their own for its own sake. But it is not unknown for them also to want one to widen a gap between their family and the stepchildren of a previous family.

Is there any answer?

The simplest is not so simple

One answer seems obvious. Until children reach maturity parents should not become involved in new relationships. If, of course, you are so inclined that is how things will turn out anyway. But that's a policy of despair for most parents, and for children despair in a parent may be as damaging as the results of finding a new partner. So obvious answers are not so simple.

More complicated solutions

If you are to find less obvious but more effective answers, you first need to consider how different *levels* of a new adult relationship may affect your children.

For example, a new male or female partner who lives away from your family is likely to cause least worry to your children. Even when very young, children understand that their parents may want and need new friends. And they do not automatically open their minds to what any such new relationship may involve – unless they actually find the two of you in bed together or otherwise too obviously wrapped around each other.

But the more time any new partner spends at your home, and the more he or she obviously makes him or herself at home in it, the more the scale of your children's anxiety is likely to rise. It will notch up significantly if your new partner moves in, or if you and your children move in with the new partner.

Yet even that's not quite the end of it.

From an early age children perceive a difference between living together and marrying. If you marry your new partner that is likely to notch your children's anxiety up a few more degrees. Adults may no longer see it this way but children still think of marriage as likely to increase the chances of their most feared prospect – that you and your new partner will have a child of your own who will wedge you apart for ever.

To understand that fear fully it helps to remember how subsequent children often spark problems with older children even when all have the same parents and live in the same family. Explaining the emotions involved to a group of mothers a child expert once put it this way:

'Imagine your feelings if one day your husband came home with a beautiful, young, blue-eyed, curvy blonde on his arm who you'd never seen before and said, "This is Sophie. She's going to live with us and we're all going to get along famously together." That is how your children can easily feel if you suddenly present them with a new brother or sister. So you have to work very hard to understand any bad behaviour which follows the birth of a new child; to keep reassuring older children; and to make sure that any feelings of rejection do not take root. If you don't you'll have endless trouble.'

If that is how the prospect of new brothers or sisters can present itself to children of the same parents, it is perhaps not so difficult to imagine how much more threatening new half-brothers and sisters may seem.

Whether you be parent or new partner you cannot avoid the impact which your relationship will have on the children; or the way their reactions are likely to affect you. So sooner or later you will have to consider:

- how your relationship will intrude on any children;
- the anxieties which it may cause;
- the seriousness of the problems you may have to face as a result;
- the extent to which you will have to pile on extra reassurance if you are to defuse those problems.

But you and your partner do have choices as to how to pitch your relationship. So it may help you to have a rough guide to the levels of anxiety which different types of arrangement are likely to cause children.

The anxiety scale

	Points on the anxiety scale
(a) Least worrying – an apparently casual new friend who calls at the house and accompanies the parent on outings.	1
(b) A little more worrying – a steady friend who visits and receives obvious signs of affection.	2
(c) A good deal more worrying – a steady friend who stays overnight but still behaves as a guest – parent and steady friend each keeping and maintaining separate homes.	3
(d) More worrying still – a steady friend who may still keep a separate home but who regularly stays overnight, and behaves as if at home.	4
(e) A cause of serious anxiety – a steady friend who moves in, the so-called common law husband or wife (but remember that common law partners have no legal status).	6
(f) A cause of very serious anxiety – marriage between parent and new partner.	8
(g) The cause of greatest anxiety – parent and new partner have children of their own.	10

Best compromises?

The least stressful compromises between the interests of parents and children are likely to lie between 1 and 4 on the scale – and these may, in fact, also offer the best short-, medium-, even long-term solutions to the problems of adjustment which parents also face after separation (see Chapter 2, pages 18–20).

But these may not be practical options. And you, your new partner or indeed both of you may want more. If you do, however, remember that although children may eventually settle to any new relationship, the higher up the anxiety scale you start, the more they will need regular and persistent reassurance if you are all to come out smiling at the end.

Dos and don'ts for parents and step-parents

First impressions are likely to set your whole future scene. They may make all the difference to any chance that you and your new partner eventually have of finding yourselves together with a new family at ease with itself.

So let's spell out some general dos and don'ts for beginner parents and new partners – and at whatever level on the anxiety scale they decide to relate:

1. Don't imagine that your children will ever accept a new partner without batting an eyelid. Perhaps the best you can hope for is that they show no reaction at the outset and reserve judgement. Curiously, the next best may be if they are hostile – at least you know that your children feel secure enough with you to make their feelings clear. But you need to be careful if they are unusually well behaved, welcoming or loving towards a new partner. Such first reactions often indicate serious anxiety and may herald real problems in the future.

2. Don't ever introduce your new partner as a new father or mother of your children, or allow yourself to be so presented if you are the new partner. Children who are old enough to remember a natural parent are not suddenly going to accept a substitute. Children who are not may bitterly resent a substitution if they later discover that there has been one. With stepchildren friendship is as much as most new partners can ever realistically hope to achieve.

3. A new partner is best addressed by stepchildren by the first or other name his or her friends ordinarily use – never daddy, mummy or similar. Stepchildren themselves may well describe a step-parent as 'My Dad' or 'My Mum' at school or when talking to their friends. But that is most often done simply to avoid the need for more complicated explanations. Don't ever imagine that it changes anything at home.

4. Don't let your children get away with any behaviour towards your new partner which you would discipline if they behaved in that way to any other visitor to your house. But make it clear to them that you are reacting only because your new partner *is* a visitor and entitled to the same manners as you expect for all visitors. On the other hand, don't demand any more of your children than that, though you will be winning if in due course they offer more.

5. If you are a new partner, do your level best to behave as you would as a guest in anyone's house while in the presence of stepchildren in their house. And treat them as you would any other guests if they are in yours – even if they do not behave as guests. Remember that well-mannered guests do not help themselves to anything without first asking or being offered by their host; and that includes answering the phone, choosing the television or video programme, and perhaps even using the bathroom. And if you are the host, remember too that well-mannered hosts first offer whatever they have to their guests – in this case the stepchildren. You may work to an entirely different set of rules when you are alone with the parent of the stepchildren. That's a matter for the two of you. But it's not likely to do any harm if you don't, and it's a lot easier to work to one set of rules.

6. Don't ask or allow your new partner to discipline your children – and if you are a new partner don't ever try, even if you have to bite off your tongue and tie your hands together to succeed. Children know full well that if there is any discipline in their home it is for their parent to dispense it. If a new partner takes disciplinary action there is a clear signal to children that he or she is out to grab the parent's role.

7. If you are a new partner don't issue orders to stepchildren or ask them to fetch or carry for you; and if you are a parent be careful, at least in the early days, about asking your children to fetch and carry for your new partner. Stepchildren will not recognise a step-parent as having any authority to order them about. And while their natural parent will normally have that authority, and may exercise it in favour of other guests, stepchildren may easily see orders from their parent in the same light as orders from a step-parent.

8. If you are a step-parent discipline yourself to stand back if children cling to their natural parent; and not to interrupt when they are talking to each other – even if they have first interrupted you to do it. And if you are a parent have a quiet word with your partner if he or she does not do this. Remember that trouble is brewing all ways round if children ever form a firm impression that a step-parent stands between them and their parent. And if you are a step-parent remember that if there ever comes a real crunch between parent, you and stepchildren, the children are ultimately likely to win.

7

Where will you live?

Months – even years – may pass before you sort out how the *ownership* of your home and its contents is to be shared between you (see Chapter 15 – or Chapter 16 if you are not married). But immediately you face separation you have to decide if either of you is to go on living in your home, and where the other is to live. These are some of the problems you may need to think about at that stage.

Will you be voluntarily homeless?

If: (a) your only chance of obtaining a home after you separate is to be rehoused by a housing association or local housing authority; and (b) you have not already been granted a tenancy of such a property, remember that, while local councils have a general legal duty to house the homeless, this does not apply to people who are *voluntarily* homeless. If you just give up or leave your home you are likely to find yourself right at the bottom of any council housing list.

So if either (or both) of you is going to need council housing you should still sit tight where you are until one of you obtains a court order for possession or transfer of tenancy against the other; or until your landlord, building society or bank obtains a possession order against you both. You are not 'voluntarily homeless' if you leave after a court has ordered you to give up possession, even if such an order is made by agreement between you. You are in any other case.

Can you afford to keep your home going – and do you want to?

If, with incomes divided after separation, you will not be able to afford to pay the rent, keep the mortgage going or otherwise maintain your home, you don't have any choices. And if neither of you wants to stay on in your previous home you don't have any problem. All you can do in either of those cases is to sell up (or give up your tenancy) and divide what's left between you – as indicated in Chapter 15 if you are married and Chapter 16 if you are not.

Large and valuable properties

If the value of your home is such that selling it is likely to produce enough to buy homes for both of you after you separate – with or without any additional funds you may have – a court is likely in the end to order that it be sold and the proceeds divided. In such cases, therefore, not least to limit legal costs, it is usually sensible to agree to sale and division of the proceeds in the first place. But if you and your partner have no children and are not married, remember that your rights to the home and its sale proceeds may be severely limited (see Chapter 16).

Homes which are to keep going

House sharing after separation

Some couples are able to agree that they will go on living in different parts of the same house long term after separation. Occasionally, people drift into that state of affairs and are then content with it – usually after both partners have slowly withdrawn into isolation and have cut off all but the most superficial contact with each other over a period of time. But many are stuck with a period of separation under the same roof because:

(a) neither has anywhere else to go or is prepared to go; and/or
(b) neither will budge without a court order and a court order is not immediately available (see below, Domestic violence cases); and/or

(c) one or other cannot afford to become voluntarily homeless (see above) and both have agreed to continue sharing the home until a court order can be obtained.

If space allows, house sharing can work, but usually only if both partners have already so distanced themselves from each other that neither cares any more for the other than for any acquaintance and that is rare. Living under the same roof is usually a recipe for an ever more miserable and stressful life for all involved.

So separation usually has to mean physical separation. And if you are married physical separation will in the end be essential if you divorce. The courts will not normally issue the Decree Absolute (which ends a marriage) unless satisfied that you are living apart (see Chapter 12, pages 85–86).

If you want to keep the stresses and legal costs of separation to a minimum you will therefore face these facts from the start and agree *who* is to go and *how* and *when* as soon as you can, and the principles governing who stays and who goes are discussed below to help you.

Domestic violence cases

Normally courts will not force either partner to leave any home which has served both of them until their property rights are sorted out (see Chapter 15 if you are married; Chapter 16 if you are not).

But if your relationship has deteriorated to the point where there is the risk of violence (or conduct approaching it) to you or your children, a court is likely to order your partner out of the house immediately. Nevertheless, such 'Ouster Orders' only give temporary protection until the rights of both of you can be decided. They do not mean that a partner who obtains an Ouster Order will then automatically keep the home, or all of its value (see Chapter 15 if you are married; Chapter 16 if you are not).

Who should go if you have children?

Owner-occupied homes

The parent who is to have day-to-day care of children is always likely to have the right to live on in any home which is to be kept going at least until the children finish at school. The children themselves (and through them the parent with their care) may have such a right to such a home if their parents are not married. And the courts are likely to follow those basic guiding lights, if asked to decide who shall retain use of the home, if that's the way the parent the children are to live with wants it.

Rented homes

If you live in a rented council or housing association house, the council or association may transfer the tenancy to any parent with care of children who is not already a tenant. In any other case the courts are likely to order a transfer of any tenancy to such a parent.

So if your children are to stay with your partner, and unless you want to risk a massive bill for legal costs by arguing about who should go, you will agree to move out, though both of you may agree to delay the move until a court order can be obtained by consent if the one who goes will face difficulty because he or she will be voluntarily homeless.

Who should go if you have no children?

If you do not have children and a court has to decide if you should be allowed to stay on in your former home (rented or owner occupied), it will consider only your and your partner's respective future needs. If separation will leave both of you in much the same position, neither of you may have any claim to stay on; if it will not, the one with greater need is likely to come out on top. If your home is rented from a council or housing association, these authorities are likely to follow similar principles in deciding whether either of you should continue as a tenant after separation.

If you do not have dependent children any decision about living on in your house is likely to follow the same principles as apply to ownership rights in it (see Chapter 15 if you are married; Chapter 16 if you are not).

Points to remember when you separate

Houses not in joint names

If the house you have been living in is owned in the name of one of you only, the other ought to see a solicitor straight away, particularly if the legal owner is the one who will be staying on in the house. You may need to take some simple but basic legal steps to make sure that your former partner cannot sell, mortgage or further mortgage the house until all money issues are properly sorted out between you; and you will need a solicitor's advice and help to do so.

Household bills

It probably didn't matter which of you actually paid telephone, gas, water, electricity, council tax and insurance bills while you were living together. But as long as such accounts remain in the name of the one who paid them, that one will continue to be legally liable for them. Once you separate that may matter quite a lot.

You are, of course, only legally liable for debts incurred in your own name and (jointly) for any incurred in joint names; but with regular running accounts you continue to be legally liable so long as such accounts remain in your name.

If you separate, therefore, you need to check all accounts which relate to any home services pretty quickly; and to make sure that they are in, or are transferred into, the name of the partner who is to remain in the home. If need be, you should also arrange for meters to be read and other records to be amended.

Notifying the relevant supplier or council is all that is usually required – and either of you can do that. But for safety's sake send them a letter and keep a copy of your letter. A telephone call may be enough. But telephone messages do get lost. Without something in writing you will not be able to prove that you have given necessary notices.

Household insurances

If you have a mortgage on your home, the property itself will usually be insured under the terms of the mortgage and that insurance will not normally change unless the mortgage arrangements do. But you should review any other household insurances, particularly any covering the contents of your home which are now to be divided between you; make sure that both of you will still be adequately insured once you part.

It is wise to ask your insurers or your insurance brokers if the change in your circumstances requires any change in your insurance arrangements.

Motor insurance and registration

If you have one or more motor vehicles be particularly careful to make sure that motor insurance arrangements and registration details will still be correct after you separate, and change them if they will not be.

Remember that:

(a) if you do not notify any change of address to your insurers or to the Driver and Vehicle Licensing Centre (DVLC) at Swansea, vital insurance and motor taxation notices may not reach you;

(b) if one of you has previously been insured under the policy of the other that one may only be insured if they drive with the consent of the policy holder, and will only then be insured if the policy holder pays the premiums. It is best if you each now have your own insurance for any car you use. Neither of you is likely to welcome loss of your no-claims bonus if the other has an accident; and neither of you is likely to want to find yourself liable to prosecution because the other has got something wrong;

(c) the person registered as keeper of a vehicle at the DVLC Swansea is the person liable for some road traffic offences. It is best if you are each now registered separately as keeper of any vehicle which you are to retain and use individually.

8

What will you live on?

If you have a job, pension or other source of independent income which will continue after separation, this obviously gives you something to help tide you over the period immediately following separation. And if you have savings of your own they too may help you over the transition.

But what do you do if these are not enough, or if you have nothing?

If you are married

If you and your partner do not already have broadly similar incomes it is almost inevitable that when your marriage is finally sorted out, the partner with the greater income and resources will be ordered to pay maintenance or make other financial provision for the one with less (for the principles see Chapter 14). But any question of such a final settlement takes time. Meanwhile the partner with the lower income may still apply to the court for maintenance to tide them over, and that maintenance will continue until any final position is reached.

So it is always sensible for anyone who is significantly better off than their partner to face the realities of maintenance from the start, and to agree to provide the other with reasonable additional support until matters are fully and finally resolved – and even if the amount of that maintenance is then made the subject of a formal consent order, usually (for convenience) in the Magistrates Courts. If that is not done the other partner may be forced to make a contested court application and that will merely increase the total of legal costs which must in the end be paid.

If you have children

If you have dependent children under the age of 17 (or 19 if still in full-time education) you have an automatic right to apply to have Child Support calculated and if need be collected by the Child Support Agency (see Chapter 13). Child Support is payable to the parent with care of children by their absent parent – the parent who no longer lives with them. But either parent can ask the Agency to make an assessment.

Child Support is payable regardless of whether parents are or ever were married, and the rules under which it is calculated include substantial maintenance for the parent with care. They thus involve a radical departure from previous principles under which an adult partner only became legally liable to maintain the other if they were previously married and the other had not remarried. Moreover, Child Support is payable regardless of any other right to financial provision: so even if you are married no other financial issue (including maintenance for you) can be considered until the amount of Child Support payable has been assessed.

Any parent who is to have care of children should therefore apply to have Child Support assessed immediately, and if the parent with care does not apply it may be sensible for the absent parent to apply – absent parents also need to know where they stand for the future.

As to Child Support, absent parents should also remember that:

(a) their liability may date from the time when the Agency sends them the form requiring details of their means – arrears may mount up if they are slow to deal with those forms;

(b) if they do not reply, the Agency can make a provisional assessment which they must pay until they supply information which allows it to be revised. Such assessments are usually set at higher figures than may eventually have to be paid;

(c) they may have to wait a long time to recover any over-payment. Small weekly deductions from future payments seem to be the rule.

If all else fails

Consult your local Department of Social Security office immediately.

If you have little or no income you will qualify for means-tested Income Support as long as you do not have savings of more than £8,000 (the value of your house and certain other assets which cannot readily be used do not come into account). If you have a job with a low income you may qualify for Family Credit to top your income up. And if you need help to pay your rent, mortgage or council tax you may qualify for Housing and Council Tax Benefit – apply to your local council for these.

If you apply for DSS means-tested benefits and have dependent children you will have to apply for Child Support or lose part of your DSS benefits – unless there are exceptional circumstances (see Chapter 13, page 89). Otherwise, you can choose whether or not to apply, though for the reasons outlined above you usually should do.

If you qualify for DSS means-tested benefits you will not have to pay any fees to the Child Support Agency, and you will qualify automatically on the means test for free legal aid – for family proceedings for which legal aid is available (all family proceedings except those for divorce itself). You will also qualify automatically for other benefits, eg free school meals for your children; free prescriptions at the chemist.

Never be afraid to apply to the DSS if you find yourself in any significant financial difficulty immediately after separation. You cannot possibly lose anything by so doing, as long as you are completely honest about details of your financial position, of course. And the only relatively sure and easy way to find out if you qualify for DSS benefits is to apply for them: you may be little the wiser if you merely read the DSS rules – they are extremely complicated.

Whatever else you do, don't try to struggle on on your own without finding out how you stand with the DSS at the earliest possible moment. If you qualify for any DSS benefit you may still only be entitled to receive it from the date you apply. There's nothing whatever to be gained by incurring debt, borrowing from family or friends, or digging yourself into any other sort of a hole simply because you have put that date off.

9

Accounts and houses in joint names – and wills

Joint accounts

Married or not many couples operate joint bank or building society accounts. They sign standing orders to cover regular payments out of these accounts. They instruct their employers to pay their salaries into such accounts.

Sometimes these accounts are opened on the basis that *both* partners must sign cheques and other banking instructions. If the couple then separate the funds in such accounts are relatively safe – both signatures are still needed.

But joint accounts are often set up so that either partner may sign. It's easier that way while you are together. In such cases both may have cheque books which allow them to draw funds independently, and both may have cards to draw cash from cash points.

Any such joint account should feature in your first thoughts if you separate, even before if you see separation coming. There's seldom much anyone can do about money which has already gone, drawn out by one partner after separation; or paid under standing orders which relate to the liabilities of only one of them after separation. And while some partners may agree not to play fast and loose with joint accounts when they separate, and may abide by those agreements, others may seize the chance to clean them out. Freeze such accounts and you can argue later – if need be in court – about which of you is entitled to any balances. But an empty account may mean that there is nothing left to argue about.

So what do you do?

1. If separation is approaching or has already occurred, contact every bank or building society in which you have a joint account and cancel your instructions for the account. Confirm your cancellation in writing and keep a copy of your letter. The account will then be frozen from the date of your notice and will stay frozen until your and your partner's rights to it are agreed by both of you or are decided by a court.
2. If you already have a separate account in your own name, sign new standing orders on that account for any payments for which you are liable and which were previously covered by the joint account; and conduct your future financial transactions through that account. If you do not have a separate account, open one.
3. Cancel any instructions to your employers to pay your salary into the joint account and give them new instructions to pay into your separate account. Think carefully whether you have previously arranged for share dividends, pension or other payments to be made into the joint account. Cancel your previous instructions and issue new ones for those as well.

These are common sense and proper steps to take in any event if you separate. So you and your partner may agree that they be taken, and may both give appropriate instructions. But do it yourself anyway unless you think there are good reasons why you should not: and even if you think there are such reasons you may still wish to have a word with a solicitor or an accountant to be sure.

Houses in joint names

'Well the house is safe. It's in our joint names.'

Such words are often spoken and in most respects they are true. If your house is in the joint names of yourself and your former partner, neither of you can sell, lease, mortgage or otherwise dispose of it or diminish its value, without the agreement and signature of the other unless a court so orders. In any such case you will know what is going on and will have the chance to object.

But that's not quite the whole story:

1. It is not unknown for people to believe that their house is in joint names when that is not the case. So have you seen the deeds?

Do you remember signing them when the house was bought? Do you know for sure that it is in joint names or are you just relying on the fact that your former partner said it was? If you are in any doubt see a solicitor straight away. There are relatively simple steps which a solicitor can help you to take to protect you until everything is clear.

2. If you have moved out of your house leaving your former partner in possession, it is quite possible for him or her to give someone else an informal tenancy without reference to the deeds, and so with no notice of your interest. If such a tenant acquires a legal right to remain in the property – as can happen – it may not be possible to sell it, or to sell it for anything like its full value. So again, see a solicitor if that might happen.

3. The final point you have to consider is what happens if you or your partner dies before everything is sorted out. There are two different types of joint ownership – as 'Tenants in Common' or as 'Joint Tenants' – and the deed putting property in joint ownership usually says which. The alternatives do not make any enormous practical difference as long as joint owners stay alive. But they make a profound difference if one of them dies:

   (a) If property is held as 'Tenants in Common' and a joint owner dies, that joint owner's share of the property passes into his or her estate and then on to whoever is entitled to inherit that estate.

   (b) If property is held as 'Joint Tenants' the share of any joint owner who dies passes automatically to the surviving joint owner.

Alternative (b) is often exactly what couples want as long as they stay together, so your deeds may well have been drawn up on the basis that you own any 'joint' property as 'Joint Tenants'. But alternative (b) is not likely to be what you will want if you separate.

So what do you do?

A joint tenancy ceases and a tenancy in common in equal shares takes its place as soon as any joint tenant serves a written notice of severance on the other joint tenant or tenants. All such a notice need say is something such as: 'I hereby give you notice severing the joint tenancy under which we previously held the property at . . . [then add a description of the property, your address, the date and your signature]'.

But if you serve such a notice it is also essential that you or someone on your behalf can later prove both that it was served and what it said. So it is almost always wise to get a solicitor's help with such notices even if you think you know how to do them yourself.

Are there any circumstances in which a severance notice should not be served?

Perhaps there are if you are minded to gamble. After all everything depends on who dies first. So if you think you are going to outlive your former partner, or if you don't care what happens to your property after you die, you may still decide to let sleeping dogs lie in the hope that in the end you will be the winner who takes all.

Now to some general questions about what happens if either of you dies before everything is sorted out.

Why wills matter on separation

Here we consider only matters you need to bear in mind at the time of separation – wills and inheritance are themselves discussed in greater detail in Chapter 19.

Your will (or the legal rules of intestate succession if you do not have one) spells out who is to have your property if you die. But your will (or those rules) does not always have the last word. Surviving partners and other relatives may have claims on an estate regardless of what wills or intestacy rules say (see 'The 1975 Inheritance Act' below and Chapter 19, pages 148–50). On the other hand, your will (or those rules) does define the most likely destiny of your property – and as your ideas about that destiny are likely to change sharply if you separate, a will or a new will is still important.

As far as inheritance is concerned the position of married and unmarried couples may be very different so we will consider them separately.

Married couples

Legally, your married status continues until a court grants a Decree Absolute of divorce or nullity (see Chapter 12, pages 85–86). If you have not made a will and die before Decree Absolute your former partner will still be your legal spouse and will still be entitled to inherit all or the main part of your estate under the rules which govern intestate inheritance (see Chapter 19, pages 147–148).

In addition, if you have made a will which includes any gift to your former partner, or appoints him or her guardian of your children or executor of your estate, those provisions will also continue to operate until Decree Absolute.

So unless you still want these things to happen, you should spell out what you now want to be the case by making a will, or by making a new one as soon as you separate.

Unmarried couples

Unmarried couples have no right to inherit anything from each other under intestacy rules. So if neither of you has made a will neither stands to receive any automatic benefit from the estate of the other before or after separation.

Not least for that reason many unmarried couples do make wills in favour of each other. But such wills remain in full force and effect unless or until they are revoked or another will is made. There is no legal cut-off as there is with Decree Absolute for the married. So if you have made a will but are no longer happy with what it says after separation, make another one which does reflect your wishes as soon as you can.

The 1975 Inheritance Act

Under the 1975 Act:

1. A surviving spouse who has not remarried (or been party to a relevant clean break divorce settlement – see Chapter 17, page 133) may apply for reasonable financial provision out of the estate of a deceased former spouse. The circumstances of all involved have to be taken into account. But if a court takes the view that the spouse should have received more than is allowed

by any will or any right to inherit on intestacy, it can award more
and so override the will or the intestacy rules.

2. All children and any surviving partner of an unmarried couple
   who previously lived together can claim reasonable financial
   provision for their *maintenance*, but surviving partners can only
   claim if the couple were still living together at the time one of
   them died. So if you and your partner were not married, forget
   about any claim under the 1975 Act once you separate. But, if
   it is not too ghoulish to say so, bear it in mind if you are merely
   thinking about separating.

3. There is a time limit on all claims under the 1975 Act. Basically,
   they must be made (ie by application to the court) within six
   months of *probate* being obtained to the will of the deceased;
   or *letters of administration* being granted to his or her estate
   (letters of administration are the equivalent of probate where
   there is no will). This time limit can only be extended in very
   special circumstances. So if you intend to claim or think you may
   have to, see a solicitor as soon as possible after the death of your
   former partner.

10

Lawyers and Legal Aid

Do you need a solicitor?

You do not have to have a lawyer to conduct your own legal case; or to make a will, transfer property or carry out any other legal function for yourself. Everyone is entitled to act as their own lawyer. And anyone who chooses to conduct their own court case – a litigant in person – is likely to receive such help as any court can then reasonably offer.

So if you decide to be a litigant in person, you can expect some help from the courts over procedural hurdles which a qualified lawyer would have to surmount unaided, and basic assistance at least from the staff in court offices in dealing with documents and procedures which have to be completed before a case goes to court.

But would-be DIY lawyers still face serious problems:

(a) Unless you know what has to be done, or done next in a court case, you are unlikely to know even when to ask for help.
(b) Unless you already know a good deal about law and the court rules and procedures, you may miss important points even if you receive general advice and help.
(c) You are too closely involved to be able to stand back and assess the realities of your own and your opponent's case objectively. An objective view is almost essential if any case is to be presented to a court effectively – and that is particularly so with family disputes which almost always involve strong personal feelings.

Lawyers have a saying which summarises this wisdom: 'He who has himself as his lawyer has a fool for a client.' And that saying was not coined just to keep lawyers in business. If lawyers find themselves in legal battles they almost always instruct other lawyers to represent them.

There are nevertheless some qualifications on these general principles in family disputes:

1. Many types of family case can be started in the Magistrates Courts (see Chapter 11, page 70). In those courts paperwork and procedures are simple and court staff play a far more active part than in other courts in seeing cases through. So you are likely to find it a good deal easier to prepare any case for a Magistrates Court, and to obtain any agreed ('consent') order in such a court. But if your case is *contested*, you will face more or less the same level of difficulty whatever court hears it.

2. Any question of maintenance for your own children now goes first to the Child Support Agency and Child Support is dealt with outside the court system altogether. All you do to apply for, or respond to, a claim for Child Support is fill in the appropriate question and answer forms and send them off with the appropriate fees to the Child Support Agency (see Chapter 13).

3. The procedure for starting and carrying forward an application for divorce has been deliberately simplified so that people can deal with divorce alone themselves. Such cases must be started in one of the County Courts (see Chapter 11, page 70). The instructions for completing the necessary forms are printed on them and County Court offices can usually supply the forms and give further advice about them.

But this simplification has not been extended to Ancillary Proceedings. Ancillary Proceedings often have to accompany divorce – for maintenance not covered by the Child Support Agency; for lump sum payments, and for property transfer, for example. You may well need help from a solicitor with Ancillary Proceedings, but you may qualify for Legal Aid if your means are limited (see below).

In general you are likely to make your life much easier if you obtain preliminary advice at least from a solicitor as soon as you realise that you are likely to have to unravel any significant family problem. However, you and your partner are then likely to save yourselves a stack of costs if you can agree all the *details* of what you want to do yourselves (Chapters 14–18 have been written to help you do that). But even if you manage to agree everything it is still wise to get a solicitor to deal finally with the paperwork for putting it into effect.

That paperwork does matter. In family cases the courts have wide powers to upset and rearrange agreements which individuals reach on their own. Indeed, between married couples no agreement is ever final and binding unless incorporated into a formal court order made after Decree Nisi in divorce or nullity proceedings (see Chapter 12, page 83). And drafting the precise terms of such orders is very much a case where skilled legal knowledge is essential.

How to find the right solicitor

Through existing solicitors

If you already have solicitors of your own they may deal with your new problems. If both of you have previously used the same solicitors they may feel that they cannot properly act for one of you against the other. But any existing solicitor not able to act for you will almost always be able to suggest one or more suitable alternatives.

Through personal or agency recommendation

Friends, relatives or any professional people known to you may well be able to recommend someone of whom they already have good experience. Citizens' Advice Bureaux – and the Law Society – will almost always be able to give you a name or names of convenient local firms with appropriate experience.

By taking pot luck

Don't ever imagine that somewhere there is a particular lawyer who is likely to be so good at his job that his skills will make a terrific difference to your chances. Family work is a mainstream activity for solicitors – it could hardly be otherwise with something approaching 170,000 divorces every year. Family law is also a field where the courts themselves actively pursue what they consider to be the right answers, often regardless of what either party or their legal representatives may say. Therefore, any firm of solicitors of any size is likely to have several staff well equipped to help you. And many smaller firms, perhaps with two or three partners, may be equally capable. These days no solicitor is likely to take your case on in the first place unless he knows that he is equipped to deal with it. Getting things wrong is too costly.

So if all else fails don't be afraid to dive into *Yellow Pages* to find a solicitor in your locality; or to go into the first solicitor's office you come across. If they can't help you they will tell you of someone who can.

How will you pay for your solicitor?

The Legal Advice Scheme

If your means are limited you may qualify for free or assisted legal advice and other general assistance (including help with completing divorce forms) under the Green Form Legal Advice Scheme. This assistance is based on a simple means test which solicitors administer. You ask your solicitor if you qualify for help under the scheme. You answer the questions he asks about your income and dependants. He then tells you straight away if you qualify and how much you must pay if you have to contribute. From then on he looks after your Green Form assistance. And he can apply to the Legal Aid authorities for its extension if circumstances make that necessary. If you qualify for Green Form assistance you will also be exempt from court fees.

The Legal Aid Scheme

Qualifications for Legal Aid

If your means are limited and you have to take or defend a case in court you may qualify for Legal Aid to cover the costs of your own lawyers acting for you. Solicitors usually carry a stock of Legal Aid application forms. So do Citizens' Advice Bureaux.

Legal Aid is subject to a far more wide-ranging means test than Green Form advice. As a result applying and waiting to see what happens is often the only way to find out for sure if you qualify. But the means test is not the only hurdle. You also have to satisfy the Legal Aid Board that, on the face of it, you have a valid case to pursue. That will almost invariably be so with any dispute involving children, maintenance or property, but it may not be so in some other types of family dispute.

In summary you will only be granted Legal Aid if:

(a) Legal Aid is available for the proceedings you wish to take – it isn't, for example, for basic divorce proceedings: you are expected to deal with those yourself, with or without help under the Green Form Scheme.

(b) You qualify under the means test rules – and pay any contribution to which an offer of Legal Aid is subject.

(c) Your application satisfies the Legal Aid Board that you have a legitimate case to pursue – though if the Board considers that it needs more information before it can make up its mind, it may first issue a certificate limited to the cost of obtaining that information.

What does Legal Aid cover?

A full Legal Aid certificate guarantees payment to your own solicitors of all the costs they properly incur on your behalf through to the completion of your case. When the case ends your solicitor presents a detailed bill to the court for scrutiny (taxation is the technical word). The amount he is entitled to is decided by taxation. So once such a certificate is granted, while it is your solicitor's job to make sure that he doesn't do work outside the certificate (for which he will not be paid), he knows that the Legal Aid Board will in the end pay him what the court agrees he is entitled to.

But is Legal Aid free?

As far as *you* are concerned, what the Legal Aid Board pays your solicitor is in the nature of a *loan* – which you may have to pay or repay.

How? As follows:

(a) If you have to pay a contribution under your certificate that contribution goes automatically towards your solicitor's costs.

(b) If you actually recover costs from your opponent those costs also go towards your solicitor's costs – but bear in mind that any such 'recovered' costs will rarely be sufficient to pay all your costs because costs rules limit what winners can recover from losers.

(c) If you recover or retain anything of value as a result of your case the Legal Aid Board also has first claim on that for any costs still outstanding after (a) and (b) above. But there are limits to that recovery in family proceedings:

- The Legal Aid Board will leave you with the first £2,500 of any winnings.
- If what you 'win' is your house, or a share in it, or money with which to buy a house, the Board will not then defeat the whole purpose of your case by insisting that you immediately sell it to pay your costs. Instead, it will put a charge (the same as a mortgage) on your house for the amount outstanding and you will only have to pay when the property is sold. But you will have to pay interest, as on any mortgage, until then.

So is Legal Aid ever free? Only if you do not have to pay any contribution and at the end of the day end up with less than £2,500. The state system spares you the problem of providing your solicitor with enough money to keep your case going until it is complete. But in every other respect you have to think as carefully about costs as people who do not qualify for Legal Aid and have to pay their own from the start.

The rest of this chapter looks at their position.

Paying for your own solicitor

If you do not qualify for state Legal Aid you will have to cover the costs of a solicitor from the start. Those costs will be the total of:

(a) his own charges for the work he does, plus VAT;
(b) any court, barristers', experts' or other fees which he has to pay on your behalf while conducting your case.

Most of your solicitor's charges will relate to the time spent dealing with your case. Seldom if ever is it possible to predict that time in advance. But from the outset your solicitor ought to be able to tell you what hourly rates he will charge for the work he and his colleagues may have to do. And he is under a professional duty to do that – as he is also to advise you about legal aid. So do not be afraid to ask; or to ask several different solicitors if you want to shop around.

If you have to pay your own costs your solicitor is entitled to ask you to deposit money with him in advance, by one or a series of payments, to cover costs as they accrue; and just as Legal Aid may be withdrawn if you fail to pay any contribution required, so your solicitor may stop work on your case if you fail to pay instalments due to him.

But your solicitor is not the final arbiter of the *total* costs you must pay. If at the end of the day you do not agree the charges he proposes, or the items of work to which they relate, you can require him to present a detailed bill for taxation by the court as he would have to in a legally aided case.

Keeping costs down

Legally aided or not, the main part of the ultimate cost of your case will come from the time your solicitors have to spend on it. So right from the start it is in your interest – and your partner's – to do all you can to limit that time.

How can you do that?

1. If it is humanly possible for you and your former partner to agree solutions to all or any of the problems which you face, do it. Any question of basic child maintenance will be sorted out by the Child Support Agency (see Chapter 13) and both of you will need to know what assessments the Agency will make before you can look sensibly at any other aspect of your financial affairs.

    There are no hard and fast rules on anything else. And if you can arrive at answers sensible to the two of you on any other issue (children; spousal maintenance if you are married; who shall have the house; in what proportions its ultimate value shall be shared, and so on) you will each save yourselves a small fortune and spare what remains of your family fortune being additionally ruined by costs.

    The ideal to aim for is that in the end you should both be able to go to solicitors and say: 'This is what we have agreed. Neither of us wants you to spend any time or money debating it with us or our solicitors. All we want you to do is prepare the right paperwork to put what we have agreed through the courts and obtain proper court approval for it.'

If you reach that ideal, stick with it.

Chapters 14, 15, 16, 17 and 18 are designed to help you towards that end, apart from explaining how the system works. But be in no doubt: divided though your family may have to be in future, it is still not in your interest or anyone else's that the resources of any of you should be eaten up by any cost which can be saved.

2. Before you see a solicitor write down a full and detailed account of all the events which have led up to your case. Start with your full name, address, post code, telephone number and date of birth. Give the same details for your former partner and any children you have. If you and your former partner were married give the date and place where you married and attach a copy of your marriage certificate. Then set out all the facts which have led up to where you are now – if possible in chronological order, starting with the earliest and ending with the latest. Give full details of your own financial position – income, savings, property and anything else which may affect it; and as much of the same detail as you may have for your partner and your children. If possible, have all this typed out double spaced on one side only of A4 paper. But if that is not possible try to write it down clearly, double spaced, and on one side only of the paper. Writing everything out will be a chore – probably a painful one. But you may save your solicitor several hours' work straight away (and yourself its cost) if you can give him such a statement when you first see him.

3. If you have letters, copy letters or other documents which may feature in your case, put them all together in date order before you first see your solicitor. Include *anything* which may have a possible bearing on your case. Don't leave out documents which you think do not matter. They may matter. Even if they do not, there may be references to them in the rest of your documents which your solicitor will then still have to check out (extra cost) to be sure.

4. If your solicitor asks for more information supply it as quickly and completely as you can. He can't take your case any further without that information and it will cost you money each time he has to write or telephone to remind you.

5. Never assume that your partner will automatically pay your costs even if you win.

   (a) If you obtain an order for costs, those costs will seldom approach what you may have to pay your own solicitor – costs rules limit what is recoverable.

   (b) In family cases courts often take the view that each side should pay their own costs, or that only a fixed and limited figure should be allowed.

   (c) No order for costs is likely if the court is satisfied that your partner cannot pay.

   (d) Even if an order for costs is made it is worthless unless your former partner actually does pay. If he or she fails to pay willingly, you can only hope to compel payment by the same court procedures – often expensive – as are available to recover debts. All too often those procedures do not work.

11

Which courts do you go to? What problems can they tackle?

The courts

Most family cases start in a Magistrates or County Court or in the Divorce Registry of the Family Division of the High Court in London. The addresses and numbers of your local courts are listed under 'Courts' in the telephone directory.

Magistrates Courts are the lowest rung in the ladder of criminal courts. But they have long had a major family role. And they now include separate Family Proceedings Courts with magistrates specially trained for family cases.

Only County Courts and the Divorce Registry can deal with claims for divorce, nullity, formal Decree of Judicial Separation, property transfer or payment of a lump sum over £1,000. And property disputes between unmarried people may have to be taken in the Chancery Division of the High Court. But County and Magistrates can both deal with most other family problems.

All family cases are dealt with in private. The media can only report words included in a *judge's* decision read in open court. All that that will amount to in an ordinary undefended divorce case is the name of the parties and the grounds on which the divorce has been granted. And no details of any case are ever likely to emerge unless there is an appeal to the Family Division of the High Court, the Court of Appeal or the House of Lords, and the decision involves important legal issues. In such cases the judges may deliver a judgment which includes relevant facts in open court. But reports will often only refer to the parties by their initials – *S* v *S*, for example.

Court officials

Cases in Magistrates Courts are decided by specially trained but legally unqualified (ie lay) magistrates, as advised on law by a legally qualified clerk.

County Court judges deal with children's cases in the County Courts. They also pronounce the formal Decree Nisi (see below) in divorce and nullity cases. But County Court Registrars, who have specialist technical and legal qualifications, deal with all procedural steps. And the Registrars also decide most financial cases, though they may refer to a judge cases of particular difficulty likely to require a long hearing.

Appeals

Any decision of a Magistrates or County Court may be appealed to a higher level. But:

1. appeal rights are subject to short and strict time limits; and
2. the principles and procedures involved in appeals are often very technical.

If a Magistrates or County Court reaches any decision which you think you must appeal, your wisest course is to see a solicitor immediately.

Cases relating to children

Basic rights

All children – natural born or legally adopted – have the same legal rights. And their parents owe the same duties and enjoy the same or similar privileges with regard to them. The marital status of natural parents is irrelevant (see Chapter 18).

But step-parents are different. If you have married someone who has children by a different parent *and* have accepted those stepchildren as members of your family a *court* (but *not* the Child Support Agency – see Chapter 13) may deal with their position and yours as if they were your natural children. On the other hand, step-parents have no special duties or rights with regard to stepchildren who have *not* been accepted as members of their family; or in any event if they have not married the parent of the stepchildren.

Residence and ongoing contact

You will best serve the interests of your children (and save substantial legal costs) if you and your partner can agree which parent your children are to live with after you separate, and what ongoing contact they are to have with the other parent (for details see Chapter 18). Then the courts will at most merely make a consent order which mirrors what you have agreed. But if you cannot agree these or any associated issues the courts will decide for you – as they also will if neither parent can or will look after the children.

Applications for consent orders or decisions which spell out parental rights, residence, contact or other detailed arrangements for children (see Chapter 18) can be made to a Magistrates or County Court. But it makes no practical difference where you begin. It's the court's job to consider whether a case raises special difficulties and to refer it to a different court if that court is better equipped to deal with them. Thus a Magistrates Court can pass a children's case to a County Court or to the Family Division of the High Court. And any of those courts can refer one to any of the others.

As a result most children's cases now start in Magistrates Courts. You only need a County Court if some other issue also arises – divorce or property claims, for example – which Magistrates have no power to deal with.

Other children's cases

Magistrates or (occasionally) County Courts also deal with other children's cases, for example:

(a) adoption;
(b) paternity – who is father of a child;
(c) local authority care.

An application to make a child a Ward of Court (see Chapter 18, page 142) may only be made to the Family Division of the High Court. But such applications are rare. Nearly all the ground they used to cover is now covered by Magistrates Court procedures. And all kidnapping (child abduction) cases now involve a criminal offence even if a parent is the kidnapper. If your child is snatched you go straight to the police and they do the rest.

Child maintenance

Any application for maintenance (regular weekly or other payments) for your *own* children must first go to the Child Support Agency (see Chapter 13). After the Agency has assessed Child Support, a County Court can consider if financial circumstances are such that *additional* maintenance should be paid – for school fees, for example (see Chapter 14, page 92). But the Child Support rules are such that additional maintenance is only likely if parents are seriously rich.

Now a cautionary word. People usually think of child maintenance as something for which *adults* apply. But since 1989 children have had the right to apply for maintenance, against either or both parents. Grants and other similar support for further education are drying up, but parents continue to be legally liable to maintain their children until they complete their full-time education. In future older children may themselves turn to the law for maintenance if parents can pay but won't.

Property and capital provision for children

A County Court, but not a Magistrates Court, can order *any* parent to transfer property to children (or to settle it in trust for them) as part of arrangements for child maintenance up to the age of 18.

Such orders are rare in favour of children of *married* parents. Their interests are usually covered by the parents' property arrangements made after divorce (see Chapters 15 & 17). But property orders in favour of children of *unmarried* parents are becoming more common. The courts have no power to rearrange the savings and property of unmarried couples just to meet their future needs. If children are likely to be left out on a limb as a result (without a roof over their heads, for example) children's rights may be used to get round the problem.

Cases involving the rights of adult partners

If you are married and separate, you and your partner have a far wider range of mutual legal rights and liabilities than if you are not married. Where you stand is therefore best examined by looking at the different problems which the courts can address and the courts which can address them.

Domestic violence

Married or unmarried, no one is expected to endure violence or the serious risk of it from any partner – to them or to any child. So under the Domestic Violence and Matrimonial Proceedings Act 1976 any partner who faces such a problem may apply to a Magistrates or County Court for an 'Ouster Order' to exclude their partner from the home they share and for such other protection as is necessary. But an Ouster Order will not be made merely because it is inconvenient or distressing still to have your partner under the same roof; and it will not decide your final rights and liabilities in your home. Those depend on your property rights if you are not married (Chapter 16) and your matrimonial rights if you are (Chapter 15) – and will be finally decided when those rights are. However, an Ouster Order will hold the fort until a court can decide those rights.

Separation orders

If you are married you can apply to a Magistrates Court for a separation order – more commonly a separation and maintenance order. But separation orders now have little practical purpose. You don't have to live with your spouse and don't need a separation order to separate. And if separation is necessary for your protection only an Ouster Order (see above) is likely to achieve what you want.

Decree of judicial separation

If your marriage has ended, neither of you wants to divorce, but you want to sort your financial affairs out finally, you can apply to the County Court for a formal Decree of Judicial Separation. Following such a decree the court can make final maintenance and property orders as it can following divorce.

There is no comparable procedure for the unmarried.

Divorce and nullity

A marriage only ends legally when one spouse obtains a final decree of divorce or nullity (Decree Absolute) against the other – or one of them dies. A Decree Absolute is only granted after the court has first granted a Decree Nisi (see Chapter 12). A Decree Nisi is a provisional decree which triggers rights to apply for final financial decisions but does not affect the legality of a marriage. You are still guilty of bigamy if you remarry before Decree Absolute.

Applications (technically Petitions) for divorce or nullity can only be launched in County Courts or their central London equivalent. Magistrates have no role in these matters. Petitions usually automatically include applications to deal with issues involving any children, adult maintenance, though some of these may be sorted out beforehand by separate proceedings in Magistrates Courts. The principles and procedures involved are considered in detail in Chapter 12.

Maintenance if you are married

Married partners have a basic legal duty to maintain each other to the extent that they cannot maintain themselves. If the income of one of you is significantly higher than that of the other, he or she is likely to be liable to pay maintenance if you separate (the principles which govern court maintenance calculations are considered in Chapter 14).

The right to maintenance continues until:

(a) there is a final ('clean break') order following divorce (see Chapter 17);
(b) the partner entitled to maintenance remarries or dies.

Permanent maintenance will only be ordered by a County Court after Decree Nisi has been granted in divorce, nullity or Decree of Judicial Separation proceedings. But if you and your partner can agree reasonable maintenance to tide you over until then you can apply to a Magistrates Court for a consent order which will run until such matters are finally sorted out. And if you can't agree you can apply to a Magistrates or County Court to decide such maintenance.

As with every aspect of family law you will save costs if you can agree (see further Chapter 14 for the principles).

Maintenance if you are not married

There is as such no right to maintenance between partners who are not and were not married. *But:*

(a) if you are entitled to claim Child Support from your partner, that support will include significant maintenance for you as parent with care (see Chapter 13);

(b) if your partner dies – *but only while you are still living together* – you have the right to claim reasonable provision for your maintenance out of his or her estate (see Chapter 19).

Savings, capital and property if you are married

A Magistrates Court can order one spouse to pay a lump sum to the other but only up to a maximum of £1,000. Any claim which involves more than that, or any question of shares in property or property transfer, can only be dealt with by a County Court and then only after Decree Nisi in divorce, nullity or formal Decree of Judicial Separation.

At that stage the courts have wide powers to redistribute assets and potential assets between spouses. But although the legal principles which govern the exercise are extremely flexible and imprecise, it is still the case that if you can first agree who is to have what (so that you only need a court consent order) you are likely to save substantial costs. Chapter 15 is designed to help you towards that.

Savings, capital and property if you are not married

The courts have no general power to redistribute property between people who have not married. You are likely to be entitled to retain anything you owned before your relationship started, plus anything you have acquired since without any financial input, direct or indirect, from your partner. You may also have some rights to any property which has been bought or is held in your joint names, though not necessarily equal rights. And if you have contributed money or moneys worth to the value or purchase of property held in the name of your partner you may have a right to claim a share in that (see Chapter 16 for details).

But the rights, if any, of unmarried couples rest on legal property principles as they apply to any two or more people who jointly buy or contribute to property. Unlike married couples the fact that you have lived together and supported each other is on its own irrelevant.

Any claim to property, or to a share in it, between unmarried couples must be made in a County Court or the Chancery Division of the High Court. Magistrates Courts have no say in such matters. But the costs of court proceedings may eat up just as much of your property as they may if married couples slog it out in court. So you and your partner will also best serve your interests if you can first agree who shall have what. And then go to court only if a court consent order is needed to implement your agreement. Chapter 16 considers the legal principles likely to apply to these problems.

12

Divorce – and a note about nullity

The right to divorce

You cannot begin divorce proceedings unless:

(a) you have been legally married for at least 12 months. It makes no difference where you married as long as the marriage was legal where it took place;

(b) you either already have your permanent home in England or Wales (Scotland has a separate legal system with its own rules); or whichever of you intends to start proceedings has lived there for at least 12 months immediately before they start;

(c) basic arrangements are in place for the residence, education, maintenance and upbringing of your own children *and* for any stepchildren accepted as members of your family – even if you or your partner intend to ask the court to change those arrangements;

(d) you have legal grounds for divorce.

The grounds for divorce

Proposals to change the grounds for divorce have been under discussion since 1990 (see Appendix, pages 151–152). But the grounds set out in the Divorce Reform Act 1969 are still likely to remain in force for most of the 1990s.

.These are the existing grounds. You are entitled to a divorce if you prove that your marriage has irretrievably broken down, ie if you prove one or more of the following facts:

(a) Your partner has committed adultery and you find it intolerable that the two of you should continue to live together (adultery); or

(b) Your partner has behaved in such a way that the two of you cannot reasonably be expected to go on living together (unreasonable behaviour); or

(c) Your partner has deserted you for a continuous period exceeding two years (desertion); or

(d) You and your partner have lived apart for a continuous period exceeding two years and you both consent to divorce (two years' separation by consent); or

(e) You and your partner have lived apart for a continuous period of at least five years (five years' separation).

But how do you 'prove' these things?

Originally the grounds for divorce had to be proved by evidence at a formal (and expensive) court hearing – and this is still so in the tiny handful of cases which are defended (less than 1 per cent of all divorces). But there is no practical purpose in defending a divorce case now because:

1. It is a fact of life that if one partner is hell bent on divorce (and has demonstrated that fact by issuing a divorce petition) no amount of time spent deciding whether he or she is entitled to it, or can provide reasons for it, is likely to make any difference to the marriage itself. Further damage to the partners and any children they have is all that is likely to result from a court battle over reasons.

2. Rules and procedures have been changed over the years to isolate divorce itself from important interests which may have to be considered with it – those of children and those involving money and property. Therefore, the reasons advanced for a divorce itself no longer make any difference to decisions about children or financial matters – though they may be raised again in proceedings over those separate issues if they affect the future welfare of children; or (in rare cases) if the conduct of one partner has had a significant effect on the future financial position of the other.

3. Defending the question of divorce alone is therefore now an enormously expensive exercise which is not likely to achieve any positive result – indeed, for this reason Legal Aid is not now granted either to bring or defend divorce proceedings themselves.

So *undefended* divorce, which has been reduced to a low-cost paperwork exercise, is now the norm. 'Proof' is by what is written in the divorce petition plus supporting documents subsequently delivered to the court. Notes on the printed forms of all the documents spell out what supporting 'proof' documents are required.

The commonest grounds for undefended divorce

More than two-thirds of all divorce cases are based on allegations of adultery or unreasonable behaviour – and more than half on unreasonable behaviour. These are the only two grounds which allow immediate divorce without proof of any prior period of separation. They are most common because people don't want to wait once they have decided they want a divorce.

But why does unreasonable behaviour have the runaway lead?

What the court has to consider in unreasonable behaviour cases is 'not whether the behaviour has been of a grave and weighty nature, but whether a right thinking person, knowing the parties and all the circumstances, would consider it unreasonable to expect the Petitioner to live with the Respondent'.

So the law is concerned essentially with what each person seeking divorce considers unreasonable. There are no specific facts to be proved, as there are with the other grounds (eg adultery or two or more years' separation). The court does not have to decide if the Petitioner's ideas of what is unreasonable also satisfy some general objective test. And it's not difficult for anyone to draw up a list of elements in their partner's behaviour which they consider unreasonable. You don't have to live with anyone very long before you have enough experience of them to be able to do that, even if it's only a matter of niggles.

Of course, if you or your partner drew up and exchanged such lists while you were still living together the chances are that each of you would immediately come up with explanations which wouldn't leave much obvious room for reasonable complaint. But this is where the second element in unreasonable behaviour petitions comes into play. Partners can only reply to anything said in a divorce petition by defending the case. And for the reasons set out in 'The grounds for divorce' above, that just is not practical.

All the courts usually ever see is the list of things which the Petitioner considers unreasonable. Lacking the Respondent's story, rarely can they do more than decide that if the Petitioner considers the stated details of the Respondent's conduct unreasonable they must be.

There is nevertheless one important piece of practical advice to add to that. It is not usually practical to defend a divorce case, however hurtful or inaccurate allegations of unreasonable behaviour may be. But if you land allegations on your partner without any prior warning this will not stop him or her feeling additionally angry or resentful. And you and your children may well pay a price for that unnecessary extra anger and resentment for years to come.

If you plan to divorce for unreasonable behaviour try to make sure – either directly or through solicitors – that your partner knows in advance, and is prepared to go along with what you propose to say. In any event don't ever turn the knife in the dying corpse of your relationship by including avoidable extreme allegations.

The procedure for divorce

Necessary forms

You can obtain standard printed divorce petition forms (each of the five different grounds has a different form) from law stationers and from most County Court offices. If you have children you can obtain the standard form for the statement of arrangements for children from the same sources. And there are printed notes on all these forms to tell you how to fill in the blank spaces. If you have consulted a solicitor he will be able to assist you with all the necessary steps.

You will need three copies of each form – one for the court, one for service on your partner and one for your own file. But as long as you get one top copy right you can photocopy the others before signing and dating them all.

You will also need your original or an official certified copy of your marriage certificate.

If your marriage was celebrated in this country, and you do not have your certificate, you can obtain an official copy if you write to the Registrar of Marriages, St Catherines House, 10 Kingsway, London WC2B 6JP; the Registrar will send you application forms and details of the fees.

Issuing the petition

When you have completed the forms you should post or take the following to your local County Court office:

(a) Your petition together with a copy for service on your partner.
(b) If you have children, the statement of arrangements for children together with a copy for service on your partner.
(c) Your marriage certificate.
(d) Either:

    (i) the fee of £40; or
    (ii) a certificate that you are exempt from fees – if you have Green Form advice from a solicitor or are receiving DSS means-tested benefits.

The court will check these documents to ensure that they are correct. If they are, it will issue the petition by recording it in the court records.

Serving the petition on your partner

The court will serve your petition and any children's statement on your partner by post. It will also send your partner a standard form of Acknowledgement of Service. Apart from confirming receipt of the Petition, your partner also has to indicate in that acknowledgement if he or she intends to contest (defend) your petition (usually the only sensible answer is 'No') or your proposals for any children or any claims in it for financial provision or costs.

The divorce cannot go any further until the court has the signed and completed Acknowledgement of Service back from your partner. Your partner may be wise to obtain advice from a solicitor before completing it. But your partner should not just ignore it. If that happens you will have to arrange for the petition to be served personally and that will add a substantial unnecessary cost which your partner may have to pay.

When the petition has been served

The court will send you a copy of your partner's Acknowledgement of Service once it has received it. If the Acknowledgement says that your partner intends to *defend* your petition a formal defence (answer) should follow within days; both of you are into an entirely different ball game, and are likely to have urgent need of a solicitor's advice.

But as long as your partner does not intend to defend you are in a position to apply for Directions for Trial – another form available from the court which you have to complete and return. You also have to send with it a sworn statement (an affidavit – again the court will help with this) as to the truth of your petition *plus* where relevant (eg if your petition is based on adultery) written evidence supporting your allegations (most commonly a note or letter signed by your partner in a case based on adultery).

The court will then check your Application for Directions. Assuming that all is well it will set your divorce case down in the undefended list and send you notice of the hearing date. If you have children it will at the same time send you details of a separate hearing (usually at a different time later on the same date) when the children's position will be considered.

The divorce hearing

No one need be present at the divorce hearing, which is entirely formal. Once your case has reached that stage the judge is likely to pronounce a Decree Nisi automatically when its turn comes in his list.

The children's hearing

Even if you and your partner have agreed all arrangements for any children the parent they are to live with must attend the children's hearing, and it is usually better if both can. If you and your partner have not agreed all the arrangements both of you must attend.

This first children's hearing is entirely informal and is usually held in a small private room adjoining the court. The only people entitled to be there are the judge, the parents and any legal representatives, although a judge may occasionally wish to talk to older children if any particular issue hangs on their views. Lawyers are not necessary if everything is agreed.

The ultimate purpose of the children's hearing is that the judge should at the end be able to say that he is satisfied:

(a) with the arrangements made for the children; or
(b) that the arrangements made are the best available in the circumstances.

In most cases where everything is already agreed by the parents he will be able to say that he is so satisfied at the end of the first hearing. But whatever the circumstances neither parent can apply for a Decree Absolute ending the marriage until he is satisfied.

From the outset the judge will have before him the Statement of Arrangements for the children which accompanied the petition. But he may wish to check matters of detail with either parent – which is why both should attend if possible. If he does not have enough information to allow him to reach a conclusion he will adjourn the case until his questions can be answered. And if there is any dispute which cannot be resolved at the first hearing, he will adjourn the case, if necessary, for a formal court hearing. If that happens court child welfare officers will be brought into the picture even if not already involved.

Property and money

Decree Nisi ('The divorce hearing' above) triggers your rights to apply to the court for a final sort-out of your financial affairs. Either of you can start that process by serving written notice (another standard form) on the other and on the court.

But if you have children, well before that time you should have applied to the Child Support Agency for an assessment of any Child Support that may be payable (see Chapter 13). No one, including the court, can make much sense of the rest of your financial position until any Child Support figures are known.

If you are wise you and your partner will also have talked about your general financial positions well before you reach this stage – either directly or through solicitors – and you may have already reached a comprehensive financial agreement (the principles discussed in Chapters 14, 15 and 17 may help you along that route). You are likely to save yourselves a small fortune in costs if you manage to do that, particularly if you can agree all the nuts and bolts between yourselves before you contact a solicitor.

If you have reached such an agreement all you need after Decree Nisi is a formal and detailed consent summons which spells out all its terms (a solicitor's help is almost essential in preparing that). You send that summons to the court, together with a statement from each of you of your financial position (yet another standard form), and the court is likely then to make an order in the terms requested by your summons without more ado.

If you cannot agree, and unless neither of you has any financial resources of substance, be prepared for a long, arduous, worrying and extremely expensive battle. Both of you are likely to have to use solicitors to help you along the way. And the cost of two sets of solicitors, each discovering and debating the fine detail of what you have, what it is worth and what either of you may be entitled to – and of going to court to decide if you still cannot agree – may swiftly escalate into thousands of pounds.

Decree Absolute

If you are the petitioner you can apply for the Decree Absolute of divorce six weeks after the date of Decree Nisi. If you do not do that within three months your partner may also apply. But if neither of you applies for some time after those periods you may have to supply further evidence to explain the delay, and to satisfy the court that you and your partner have not got back together again, before Decree Absolute will be granted.

You apply by completing and sending another standard form to the court together with the fee (£15) – but you do not have to pay that if you have already lodged a fee exemption certificate (see 'Issuing the petition' above).

Decree Absolute signals the legal end of your marriage and ends any rights you previously enjoyed as a spouse – pension, inheritance and widow's benefit rights are examples. After Decree Absolute you are also free to remarry.

But remember this. If you remarry you automatically lose any further right to maintenance from your former spouse. And you also then lose any further right to apply for lump sum, property transfer or other capital provision. So it is absolutely vital that you start proceedings for any such provision before you remarry. For safety's sake discuss any remarriage plans with a solicitor beforehand.

Summary of the stages in undefended divorce

1. Prepare and take divorce petition and documents to court.
2. Acknowledgement of Service (sent out by the court).
3. Prepare and take Application for Directions to court.
4. Notice of date of Decree Nisi and any children's hearing (sent out by the court).
5. Decree Nisi and any children's hearing (at the court).
6. Prepare and take Financial Provision Applications to court.
7. Apply for Decree Absolute.

How long? About three months from start to Decree Absolute if you and your partner deal with all documents immediately. But *disputed* financial applications (6. above) may run on a year or more after that.

Nullity

There are two classes of marriage to which the word 'Nullity' may apply:

1. *Void* marriages – marriages which were illegal from the start and so never existed. This category includes bigamous marriages; some (but not all) polygamous marriages; marriages celebrated when a partner was under the age of 16; marriages in which both partners are of the same biological sex; and marriages in which the spouses are within the legally prohibited degrees of relationship.
2. *Voidable* marriages – marriages which have full legal effect unless or until a court pronounces a Decree of Nullity. This category includes marriages which have never been consummated; marriages to which either party did not or could not consent because he or she was forced into it or was mentally deficient or ill; and marriages celebrated when, unknown to one partner, the other was pregnant by someone else or was suffering from a venereal disease in communicable form.

If necessary (for example, to clarify legal status) a court may declare a void marriage a nullity. But because such a marriage never had any legal existence neither partner has rights against the other under matrimonial law. But if a Decree of Nullity is granted in respect of a voidable marriage the partners have effectively the same rights and duties as they would after divorce.

It matters not as far as children are concerned whether their parents were unmarried or their marriage was valid, void or void-able. Children have exactly the same legal rights against their parents whatever their parents' status.

But nullity cases are now rare. *Void* marriages only ever constitute a tiny handful of the total number of marriages. As for *voidable* marriages, most can be more easily, painlessly and cheaply ended by divorce. Nullity procedure has not been simplified as divorce has. Nullity may still be preferred by those who have a religious or other objection to divorce. But if annulment is an available option and you and your partner prefer it you are likely to need help and advice from a solicitor from the start.

13

Maintenance:
The Child Support Agency

Published on 23 January 1995, the White Paper 'Improving Child Support' proposed many changes to the Child Support system. They will not affect any calculation of Child Support (or arrears accumulated) for periods before April 1995. And they will only have legal effect if later built into legislation – which may span several years.

The text which follows therefore covers both the White Paper *proposals* (heralded in each case by the words 'After April 1995' or 'After 1996/97' – which are the intended effective dates) and the previous position. But bear in mind that you can only rely on the White Paper elements after the dates stated – and then only if the government has not changed its mind before bringing them into force.

That said, one of those elements should be noted here. After April 1995 a parent liable to pay Child Support *may* be allowed a reduction in the weekly liability if he or she transferred property to the Parent with Care of children April 1993. This will only happen if *half* the value of the transfer (*valued at date of transfer*) was greater than £5000 and the allowance will be of a fixed amount, geared to whether the half value lay in the £5,000–£9,999, £10,000–£25,000, or above–£25,000 bands (the White Paper suggests weekly allowances of £20, £40 and £60 respectively). After 1996/97 *either* parent may then seek further discretionary review of these allowances, *up* or *down* (see 'Discretionary appeals', pages 102-103).

About the Child Support Agency

The Agency will feature prominently in your financial future if you live in the United Kingdom and:

1. you are a parent – father, mother or legal adopter – of a child here; or
2. you have married or are living with such a parent; or
3. you have care of a child here for such parents.

The Agency will continue to influence your affairs as long as any such child is under the age of 16, and after then up to the age of 19 if the child has not married and is still in full-time education. Such children are described as 'qualifying children'.

If you apply for or receive Income Support or other means-tested DSS benefit you will have to apply through the Agency for Child Support unless you can convince it that you or any child living with you may, as a result, suffer harm or undue distress. You will have to apply in any case if you want someone else to decide how much child maintenance you should receive or pay. But even if you and your partner plan to agree child maintenance privately, neither of you can afford to ignore the Agency. No agreement or court can exclude the right of either of you *at any time* to ask the Agency to decide what Child Support must be paid. So neither of you can look realistically at any other aspect of your financial affairs until you both know what the Child Support bill will be.

However, if you were already receiving DSS means-tested benefits before April 1993 and the Agency has not already taken your case on, it will not now do so unless (some time after April 1995) the government decides the Agency can and should do so. Until any such time you will qualify for DSS benefits as before.

You can obtain the Agency's free introductory guide 'For Parents Who Live Apart' from Post Offices. You can obtain forms and all necessary details by contacting the Agency direct by letter or telephone at The Child Support Agency, PO Box 55, Brierley Hill, West Midlands DY5 1YL, telephone 01345 133133.

About Child Support generally

Child Support is payable by parents who live apart from qualifying Children ('absent parents') to those who live with them ('parents with care'). It is calculated on a weekly basis, but may be paid by monthly or other instalments if agreed.

Generally absent parents are legally liable for the full amount of any Child Support assessed against them from the time they receive the Agency's form demanding information about their means; or (after April 1995) eight weeks after that date if the absent parent replies within four weeks.

But absent parents with second families who are *already paying* child maintenance *under arrangements made before 5 April 1993* only pay the full amount of any *increase*:

1. After two years if Child Support exceeds £60 a week. These are the intervening stages:

    (a) First six months – existing payment plus a quarter of the extra or £20, whichever is more.
    (b) Second six months – existing payment plus half the extra or £40, whichever is more.
    (c) Third six months – existing payment plus three-quarters the extra, or £60, whichever is more.
    (d) Thereafter the full amount.

2. After one year if Child Support is less than £60 a week but more than £20 above the existing arrangement. In such a case the increase on existing payments is limited to £20 for the first year.

If absent parents were paying maintenance under a court order or maintenance agreement before April 1993 and the Agency has not already taken their case on, it will not now do so until after 1996/97 at the earliest. Meantime the courts will continue to deal with their cases as if the Agency did not exist. But after April 1995 Parents with Care may be allowed to ask the Agency to *collect* such maintenance (subject to payment fees – see page 93 below) if it is not being paid.

The different roles of the Agency and the courts

1. On any question of how much an absent parent must pay the Agency comes first. If Child Support is payable it will therefore affect anything else which you or the courts then can or should do. Before anyone can make *any* other financial decision on family finances they first have to consider the partners' overall financial positions. And that cannot be done until everyone knows by how much Child Support will reduce an absent parent's income and resources and increase those of the parent with care.

    Moreover, while Child Support has an obvious bearing on parents' incomes, it may also affect their respective savings and capital.

    Because the legal liability to pay Child Support is geared to the time the Agency sends out the form which requires absent parents to supply details of their means, some time may pass before Child Support is assessed; and the amount assessed may be more than has been paid in the mean time. For these reasons assessments for ongoing Child Support often also include demands for lump sum arrears, and these debts for arrears inevitably change the balance between the parents' respective savings.

2. Child Support includes substantial provision for support of the parent with care as well as for the qualifying children. The rules for calculating the amount of Child Support payable take some account of the respective incomes of both parents. But, basically, as long as absent parents are liable to pay Child Support they will also contribute to the support of parents with care – even if they would not be liable to maintain them under the general law. The status of the parents – married, remarried or never married – makes a substantial difference to adult maintenance rights in the courts. But it makes no difference to the amount of Child Support.

3. The Agency cannot deal with any financial problem except that of Child Support. All other financial issues which follow separation must be resolved in or through the courts.

    So it is only through court procedures that one party to a marriage may be ordered:

(a) to pay maintenance to the other – adult maintenance;
(b) to pay a lump sum, or make a property transfer or other property provision to or for the other;
(c) to pay maintenance to or for a stepchild (ie a natural child of the other parent) accepted as a child of the family.

And it is only through court procedures that:

- any parent (married or not) may be ordered to pay a lump sum, or make a property transfer to or for the benefit of a child, or pay maintenance for a child additional to Child Support.
- property or money disputes of unmarried couples can be resolved.

The mechanics of Child Support

Who applies?

1. If you have qualifying children living with you – normally they will be your own, but other relatives with their care may also apply – you may, as parent with care, apply to have Child Support assessed against their absent parent.

   If you apply for DSS social security benefits – Income Support, Family Credit or Disability Working Allowance – you *must* apply; and you must then cooperate with the Agency in pursuing the application, or risk losing part of your DSS benefits. You are only spared that risk if you can satisfy the Agency that you or any child living with you may suffer harm or undue distress if the Agency takes action on your behalf.

2. If you are an absent parent you also may apply for a Child Support assessment. You may think that you are inviting trouble if you do. But you also need to know what your future Child Support liabilities are; and you may face additional problems if the parent with care is slow off the mark and an assessment is not available when you or your advisers need it.

How do you apply?

1. Write or telephone the Agency (PO Box 55, Brierley Hill, West Midlands DY5 1YL; telephone 01345 133133) for the

forms and information leaflets appropriate to your case. The application form is 36 pages long, requires a vast amount of information, and you will receive detailed notes from the Agency to guide you. But if you still need help solicitors, accountants or Citizens' Advice Bureaux may be able to help you.
2. Complete the form and return it to the Agency.

What fees are payable?

(a) Parents who ask the Agency to collect court maintenance (if so permitted after April 1995) will have to pay its collection fees (currently £34 a year).
(b) After April 1995 all other fees are suspended and the service will be free until April 1997.
(c) Subject to that, the general picture is that:

1. No fees are payable if you have to apply because you are receiving means-tested Social Security benefits, or are an absent parent receiving any of those benefits, or are under 16 years of age.
2. Otherwise parents with care pay £44 if they want the agency to assess the amount of Child Support; £78 if they want it to assess the amount *and* collect it on their behalf (these fees – or any substituted for them – are then payable annually until Child Support ceases to be due). In addition (and unless exempt (see 1(a) above)) absent parents pay the same fees as parents with care. Absent parents who are not exempt still pay if the parent with care is exempt.

Who decides?

The Agency's assessments are made by one of its Child Support Officers. A person dissatisfied with such an assessment may ask for it to be reviewed by another officer, and may appeal to the independent Child Support Appeal Tribunal set up under the Act if still not satisfied. But that is the end of the defined rights of appeal. Initially, any such appeal was only likely to succeed if it could be shown that the rules had been incorrectly applied. The fact that the rules produced bizarre results was not a ground of appeal. But after 1996/97 *both* parents will have limited rights to ask for a further discretionary review of Child Support calculated under the fixed rules (including those added after April 1995) – see 'Discretionary appeals' pages 102–103.

When the Agency has received the application

1. If you do not know your former partner's address the Agency will attempt to trace him or her – and it can refer to National Insurance and Inland Revenue records which are not available to you or the courts.
2. Once your former partner's address is known the Agency will send him or her an equally detailed form requiring full details of his or her position.
3. If you are that former partner remember that your liability to pay any Child Support eventually assessed runs from the date when the Agency sends you that form unless (after April 1995) you reply within four weeks. In that event your liability will run from eight weeks after that date.
4. If your former partner does not complete and return the form the Agency will estimate Child Support on the information you have given and will issue a provisional assessment. A provisional assessment is likely to fix Child Support at a higher level than may be calculated once the Agency has full information – deliberately to force your former partner to reply. But provisional assessments are legally effective, and Child Support is payable in accordance with them, unless or until the Agency receives sufficient information to revise them.
5. If your former partner overpays under a provisional assessment he or she may only be able to recover the overpayment by small deductions over a long period – £1.49 per week over 18 years in one reported case. Absent parents should remember this.

How is Child Support calculated and assessed?

The basic picture

The first objective of the law which governs the Agency is to ensure that, wherever possible, parents with care do not end up having to rely on DSS Income Support. So the basic target figure for Child Support – 'the maintenance requirement' – is calculated by working out how much DSS Income Support parents with care would be entitled to if they received no maintenance from absent parents and had no income of their own.

The question of whether that target can actually be met depends on 'the assessable income' of each parent. Assessable income is what is left after defined financial liabilities and expenses have been subtracted from the parents' total gross incomes.

The amount payable is then decided by allocating legally fixed percentages of assessable income to Child Support.

Table 13.1 gives the basic picture in diagrammatic form.

Table 13.1. *Summary of basic steps in Child Support calculation*

(A) Income calculation

1. Calculate parents' total *gross income* from all sources

Deduct

Tax, National Insurance, and half pension payments

Result

2. Total *net income*

Deduct

exempt income

Result

3. *Assessable income*

(B) Child Support calculation

1. Calculate the *maintenance requirement*

2. Child Support is *half* of assessable income up to the point where that half equals the maintenance requirement; *plus* 15 per cent, 20 per cent or 25 per cent (depending on the number of children) of any balance of assessable income above that so required. But after April 1995 the total will be limited to a maximum of 30 per cent of absent parents' assessable incomes (33 per cent if payments also cover arrears).

The following sections deal with the detail involved in working out the elements of the calculations.

The maintenance requirement

The maintenance requirement is the basic target figure for Child Support. It is the total of the following DSS Income Support allowances (usually reviewed annually) less basic Child Benefit (formerly Family Allowance):

(a) The age-related child allowance for each child.
(b) The Family Premium.
(c) As long as at least one child is under 16, a proportion at least of the adult Personal Allowance – 100 per cent until the youngest child is 11; 75 per cent until the youngest is 14; and 50 per cent until the youngest reaches 16.
(d) The Lone Parent Premium – unless the parent with care is living with a new partner.

Using 1994 rates the Agency's publication 'A Guide to Child Support Maintenance' gives the following example for two children aged 9 and 12 living in a single parent family:

1. DSS Child Allowances	£38.65
2. Family Premium	10.05
3. Lone Parent Premium	5.10
4. Adult Allowance	45.70
Total	99.50
5. Less Basic Child Benefit (£10.20 for first child; £8.25 for second – additional one parent benefit is not deducted)	18.45
Maintenance requirement	81.05

Note that part of items 2. and 3. and all of item 4. consist of maintenance for the parent with care and not the children.

Assessable income

The Agency uses the information supplied by both parents to calculate their weekly assessable incomes. These are the steps involved in that calculation:

(a) *Calculate each parent's weekly net income*
1. Add up the parent's total *gross* weekly income from all sources.
2. Deduct from that total the amount which that parent has to pay weekly by way of income tax and National Insurance contributions plus *half* of any superannuation or pension contributions payable.
3. Weekly *net income* is what remains.

(b) *Calculate each parent's weekly exempt income*
Exempt income is the amount which the regulations say a parent must retain to cover his or her own basic living expenses. Exempt income is the total of the following:

1. The DSS Income Support Adult Personal Allowance (£45.70 a week in 1994); *plus*
2. The DSS Income Support Disability Premium and Severe Disability Premium if the parent is disabled; *plus*
3. *If* the parent concerned has a child living with him or her *of which that parent is father or mother* the DSS Family Premium, plus the DSS Income Support Personal Allowance appropriate to a child of that age, plus the appropriate DSS Disabled Child Premium for a disabled child. *But*:

   - these deductions are *halved* if the parent lives with a new partner, the child is the fruit of the new partnership, and the new partner has a net income greater than the total of *that* partner's Income Support allowances;
   - there is no allowance for children of whom the parent is not father or mother, eg stepchildren; *plus*

4. If the parent concerned has a child who qualifies under 3. above but no new partner living with him or her, the DSS Income Support Lone Parent and Carer Premiums; *plus*
5. The amount of the parent's *reasonable* weekly costs for housing the parent and any of that parent's own children living with him or her, eg rent, mortgage repayments, payments for residential care etc. *But*:

   - subject to some exceptions housing costs of an absent parent are regarded as unreasonable if they exceed £80 a week *or* half that parent's net income (whichever is greater);

- even if reasonable, absent parents were only allowed the full amount of their housing cost if they lived alone or alone with children of which they were father or mother. In all other cases absent parents were only allowed to deduct a fixed percentage of their housing cost, the percentage being determined by who else shared the accommodation. For example, a remarried absent parent was allowed 75 per cent of housing costs if there were no children; 82.14 per cent if there were two children of which that parent was father or mother; but only 53.57 per cent if there were two stepchildren. After April 1995 reasonable housing costs will not be reduced because of new families. But after 1996/97 *either* parent may ask for further discretionary adjustment of housing cost allowances (see 'Discretionary appeals' page 102–103). *Plus*:

6. After April 1995 *employed* (but not self-employed) parents will be allowed 10p for every mile by which their weekly journey to work (calculated by measuring a straight line between home and work) *exceeds* 150 miles. After 1996/97 *either* parent may seek further discretionary adjustment of any such allowance; and absent parents may ask for a discretionary allowance to cover excessive costs of travel needed to maintain contact with their children (see 'Discretionary appeals' page 102–103).

(c) *Subtract exempt income from net income*
Assessable income is left.

Parents' contributions to Child Support

(a) If a parent with care has no assessable income and the absent parent's assessable income is not more than *twice* the maintenance requirement, the Child Support payable by the absent parent is *half* his (or her) assessable income.

(b) If the parent with care has no assessable income and the absent parent's assessable income is *twice or more* than the maintenance requirement the Child Support is:

- the amount of the maintenance requirement; *plus*
- 15 per cent of the amount by which assessable income exceeds twice the maintenance requirement if there is one

child; 20 per cent for two children; and 25 per cent for three or more.

(c) If both parents have assessable incomes these are added together. If the total is less than twice the maintenance requirement the Child Support payable by the absent parent is half his (or her) assessable income, as it would be if the parent with care had none.

If the total is more than that, the absent parent contributes to the maintenance requirement in the same proportion as his (or her) assessable income bears to that of the parent with care. But if *twice* the amount of that contribution does not use up all the absent parent's assessable income, he or she then also pays 15 per cent, 20 per cent or 25 per cent of the rest (depending on the number of children) regardless of the relationship between the two assessable incomes. Note that:

- Where assessable income exceeds that required to cover the maintenance requirement, the percentages of assessable income then added (15 per cent, 20 per cent or 25 per cent) also include an element of adult maintenance.
- After April 1995 all figures are capped to a *maximum* of 30 per cent of absent parents' assessable income (33 per cent if payments also cover arrears).

Under the rules an absent parent with an assessable income of £2,000 a year might still nevertheless end up having to pay nearly £500 a year Child Support to a parent with care of three children with £50,000 a year, though with such an imbalance a court might order the parent with care to pay maintenance to the absent parent (see Chapter 14 page 115).

These rules are infernally complicated, however hard one tries to set them out. An illustrative example may make it a little easier to understand how they work:

Suppose:

- Peter is an absent parent with an assessable income of £150.
- Mary (parent with care) has an assessable income of £50 (ie there is a 75 per cent:25 per cent split).

- The maintenance requirement for one child in Mary's care is £80.

The Child Support figures would work out like this:

Peter's 75 per cent of the maintenance requirement is £60. (That £60 has used up the first £120 of Peter's assessable income since he has to pay half of his assessable income until the maintenance requirement is cleared). That leaves £30 of his assessable income liable to additional assessment at 15 per cent for one child which is £4.50.

Peter's total Child Support assessment would be £64.50. Mary's 25 per cent 'contribution' would be masked by the fact that she simply retains the full amount of her own income.

Cut-off rules

(a) *Poverty trap avoidance*

Absent parents. It was realised that if Child Support was calculated as explained above on pages 94–99 the income of absent parents with new families might fall below basic DSS subsistence levels.

So the rules also include what is intended to be a safety net – the absent parent's weekly protected income. That protected income is the total (weekly) of the following:

1. £30; plus
2. The allowances for which the absent parent and all those dependent on that parent in his or her household – (including any stepchildren) would qualify if drawing Income Support; plus
3. Any part of the household's reasonable housing costs which does not arise from mortgage repayments.
4. The household's Council Tax liability.
5. If the absent parent's whole family income exceeds the total of 1. to 4. above, 15 per cent of the excess.

If a Child Support assessment would otherwise leave an absent parent and that parent's current family with less than his or her protected income, the assessment must be reduced until the protected income is intact.

Parents with care. Original Child Support rules offered nothing to parents with care who still had to rely on DSS means-tested benefits – the DSS took the lot. After 1996/97 such parents will be credited with the amount of Child Support actually paid – up to a *maximum* of £5 a week. If they then start working for more than 16 hours a week they will be able to claim payment of any accumulated credit.

(b) *Absent parents with high incomes*

It was also realised that there might be wild results if there was no limit to the incomes of absent parents on which Child Support was calculated. Therefore there is an upper limit on the amount of assessable income on which additional Child Support (at the rate of 15 per cent, 20 per cent or 25 per cent depending on the number of children) can be charged.

That limit was calculated by adding together the current Family Premium and the (age dependent) Personal Allowance which would be allowed for the qualifying children on Income Support – and multiplying the total by three.

But there were very few cases where that limit was reached. At 1994 rates, for example, the allowance for a child aged between 11 and 15 was £27.50 and Family Premium was £10.05. Therefore, the maximum weekly Child Support which could be assessed on top of the maintenance requirement for a single child in that year was £112.65–£5,857.80 a year. To reach that maximum (at a 15 per cent deduction rate) an absent parent would have to have an assessable income (on top of the portion needed to cover the maintenance requirement) which exceeded £39,052 per annum – and more if there were more children.

From April 1995 the maximum is to be halved but it is clear that there will still not be many cases where the maximum is reached. Seriously rich absent parents may still be ordered to pay more in the courts.

Special cases

(a) *Children in care of neither parent*

Child Support may be assessed against both parents if third parties have care of their children. Lone Parent Premium is excluded from the maintenance requirement if the child is in institutional care but otherwise all calculations are made as in any other Child Support case.

(b) *Children dividing time between both parents*
Child Support may be adjusted proportionally if a child spends at least 104 nights a year (two nights a week) in the household of the absent parent, but there is no adjustment for lesser periods.

(c) *Children of the same parent in the care of different people; and of different parents in the care of the same person*
Child Support may also be adjusted if the children of the same absent parent are in the care of different people; or if the same parent with care is looking after the children of different absent parents. But such cases are rare and their detailed implications are best established by direct contact with the Agency.

Discretionary appeals

After 1996/97, officers of the Agency (and on appeal the Child Support Appeal Tribunal) will have a limited discretion to bend the rigid Child Support rules in certain defined cases so as to allow for exceptional circumstances.

Absent parents will be able to seek relief if they face hardship because the formulae do not adequately take account of:

(a) Travel costs to work or to maintain contact with a child.
(b) Expenses resulting from illness or disability.
(c) Exceptional costs of caring for a step-child.
(d) Debts incurred before separation.
(e) The value of property transferred before April 1993.
(f) Obligations which were taken on because it was assumed that a maintenance agreement made before April 1993 would govern the future circumstances of the parents.
(g) Any of the matters for which a parent with care can seek adjustment under (ii)–(iv) below.

Parents with care will be able to seek similar relief if:

(i) They are not allowed sufficient deductions in respect of any of the matters allowed to absent parents (a) to (f) above.
(ii) The absent parent has assets or an extravagant life style which belie assessed income.
(iii) The absent parent can in fact afford housing costs, or has deliberately inflated them, or has a new partner who could or

should be able to meet or help with them.

(iv) The absent parent is able to meet travel costs or has deliberately inflated them.

(v) Any allowance for property transferred is too generous.

How is payment enforced?

(a) Until payment absent parents are liable to pay interest on any arrears of Child Support which have accumulated. After 1996/97 a system of penalties for late payment is to be substituted for interest.

(b) If an absent parent fails to pay Child Support the Agency can order his employer to deduct it from his wages and pay it direct.

(c) If he is not employed, or a deduction order is not effective, the Agency can apply to the courts for a Liability Order for what is due. The Agency's assessments cannot then be challenged in court. The court must accept the Agency's figures.

Liability Orders may be enforced by any of the procedures available for recovering court judgment debts. But if an absent parent has nothing those procedures are no more likely to produce results in Child Support cases than they do in any other.

14

Maintenance:
The courts and the general law

Who can claim court maintenance?

The following may claim, or be liable to pay, maintenance in the Magistrates or County Courts if they separate or divorce:

1. *Husbands and wives* – more commonly husbands have to maintain wives; but it may go the other way if a wife's income is higher than a husband's.
2. *Married parents and step-parents* – step-parents may have to maintain stepchildren previously accepted as part of their family; but usually only to the extent that other support is not available – Child Support from a natural parent for example.
3. *Parents and children* – provided Child Support has already been assessed by the Child Support Agency (see Chapter 13) the courts *can* order a parent to pay *additional* child maintenance to the parent with care, or to make some other provision – by payment of school fees, for example. But such orders are only likely against parents with substantial incomes.

Children may also apply independently for maintenance from either or both of their parents. Such orders are only likely to be made in favour of children over 18 who are still in full-time education.

How long must maintenance be paid?

1. Between husbands and wives the right to receive maintenance continues until:

(a) a County Court ends that right after divorce by making a clean break order. Clean break orders are usually made by consent but the courts can impose them without agreement if satisfied that they are right in the circumstances (see Chapter 17).

(b) the maintained partner remarries or dies.

2. Between parents and children the obligation to maintain runs until the child reaches the age of 17. But if a child continues in full-time education after that age and has not married, a parent with its care, or the child itself, may apply to the court to extend maintenance until either of those conditions ceases to apply.

3. The *amount* of maintenance may be varied (increased or decreased) on application to the court by either partner if either partner's financial circumstances change after the date of the previous order.

How is maintenance calculated?

The general picture

In the courts maintenance is seen as a means of reducing differences between the incomes of spouses (or spouses plus children if there is a family) after spouses separate into different households.

So the courts are unlikely to order any maintenance of substance between spouses without children who already have separate incomes which are approximately equal. And where incomes are not equal the courts are unlikely to order maintenance beyond amounts which will top up the income of a partner with a lower income towards an approximately equal share of joint income.

They may, however, go beyond equality (perhaps as far as a 60 per cent–40 per cent split of joint income) in favour of a spouse who also has care of the children.

Usually, both spouses are likely to be worse off after separation. In such circumstances a rough carve-up is all any court can sensibly aim for. Any more and partners who had to pay would be likely to default wholesale. Getting money out of a spouse who refuses to pay is something of a nightmare.

In the handful of cases where spouses are so rich that there is enough to allow both to preserve the standard of living they enjoyed while they were together, the courts have always applied a top limit to maintenance. In such cases maintenance is never likely to be more than will allow a partner entitled to maintenance to preserve his or her previous standard of living. Therefore, at most maintenance exists to compensate the 'poorer' partner, not to make him or her better off. But those who are rich can usually find the price for a final deal. These days rich people's cases almost always end with a clean break settlement and no ongoing maintenance (see Chapter 17).

For all that, the law does not lay down any hard and fast rules as to how courts and lawyers should set about these exercises, nor does it set up any precise target figures as it does for Child Support (Chapter 13). So in theory at least there is almost endless scope for you and your partner to argue about how much should be paid; and for both of you to ruin yourselves if you employ solicitors to argue for you, or end up asking a court to decide.

The sections which follow therefore describe how any lawyer or court *might* set about the task. Perhaps, with the help of those sections, you and your partner will be able to work out and agree your own figures for yourselves. If you can you will save yourselves a great deal of money. Employing a solicitor at the end, merely to prepare a formal consent summons, will only cost a fraction of the amount involved if you each have solicitors working out (if need be in court) the figures which end up in such summonses.

But if you agree figures remember that solicitors are still legally obliged to advise unless told not to, and if either of you wavers as a result of such advice you will be back on the costs treadmill. If you arrive at figures which make sense to you, you should both be resolute. Tell your solicitors what you have agreed. Insist that that, and no more, is what they must put in place.

Your incomes

No maintenance calculation can start until you have full and complete details of each partner's total gross income – and of the deductions which the courts will generally allow from that income to arrive at net income. Maintenance is calculated on net income.

It is usually best to start with annual figures, even if weekly or monthly maintenance is ultimately calculated from them.

(a) Annual gross income – actual income

Your actual annual gross income is the total income you receive from all sources before tax, National Insurance, pension or other deductions.

If you are employed your annual P60 tax form or your employer is likely to provide precise figures. If you are self-employed your annual tax assessment, accounts, accountant or tax inspector will usually do the same. But if your earnings fluctuate you ought to take an average over more than a year – typically three years for the self-employed.

To your earnings you should then add any other income:

- bank, building society and National Savings interest;
- share dividends, rents, trust income or pension receivable;
- any Child Support assessed in your favour – whoever may be liable to pay it;
- Family Allowance payments and any other social security benefits which are not means tested (maintenance will affect means-tested benefits so they should not be included).

If tax has already been deducted from any of these payments before you receive them (eg interest and dividend payments) you can add in the net figures as long as you do not also include the tax deducted when you calculate net income – see (d) below.

(b) Annual gross income – presumed income

Unfortunately, income actually receivable does not always complete the picture. Courts may decide that spouses are better off than their actual incomes suggest if satisfied that:

- a spouse has deliberately massaged income to keep it below normal until maintenance is sorted out; or
- accounts or other figures do not tell the whole story – a spouse has held something back; or
- a spouse has someone living with him or her (a working child or a new partner, for example) whose own income exceeds that needed to support themselves; and who, as a result, either does, could or should contribute towards the spouse's living costs.

In such cases courts are likely to add an estimate of presumed additional 'income value' to the income of the relevant spouse.

If any of these circumstances is relevant to you or your partner it may well be that you will be unable to agree how much difference they make, and will be doomed to the cost of fighting it out in court. But even in such cases it still pays to be realistic and to agree and add in figures for presumed additional 'income value' if you can.

(c) Total annual gross income

The annual gross incomes which concern you and your partner are in each case the total of your respective figures under (a) and (b) above.

(d) Annual net income

The courts have made it clear that maintenance calculations should be based on net incomes, ie gross incomes reduced by specific deductions. And although no single court has ever spelled these deductions out comprehensively, they certainly go beyond those now laid down by law for calculating Child Support (see Chapter 13, pages 96–98)

Some time ago, however, a legal consensus based on wide general experience did produce a list of the deductions which the courts will allow – and Child Support should now be added to that list. The list is as follows:

- the income tax payable by each of the parties on all income not already listed at after tax levels in the gross income calculation;
- the National Insurance contributions payable by each of the parties;
- the travel costs they have to pay to work;
- any pension or superannuation contributions they have to pay;
- any Child Support which they have to pay – to the other partner or anyone else;
- the mortgage interest or rent, and Council Tax and water charges which they have to pay for their own accommodation – but only to the extent that these are reasonable in the parties' joint circumstances. Neither you nor your partner ought to expect a court (or each other) to agree full deduction of such charges if either of you has inflated them by moving into accommodation which is excessively costly.

If you have new dependent children some further deduction – possibly limited to the allowances which would be made for them on Income Support by the DSS – may also be appropriate for them, but see paragraph (e) below on this subject.

You each arrive at your annual net incomes by deducting the total of the above deductions from your annual gross incomes worked out under paragraphs (a), (b) and (c).

(e) Additional dependants

What if either of you has new dependants?

The courts are likely to add some notional element to your gross income if you have someone living with you who is able to contribute to your household expenses. And they are likely to allow some deductions (see (d) above) from your available net income if you have children by a new partner, since you have a legal duty to support them.

But they are far less likely to allow deductions merely for new adult partners who are dependent. People who separate are free to acquire new adult partners, but if they do the common view seems to be that they do so entirely as a matter of choice. Expensive or not, choices made after separation are usually ignored and are not allowed to affect maintenance.

Calculating maintenance

Once you have your annual net income figures you and your partner can turn to working out the actual figures for the maintenance (if any) which one of you should pay the other.

But to do that you will have to rely almost exclusively on practical rules of thumb developed by the courts over many years, and not on anything laid down by law.

(a) What the law says

The only wisdom the law contributes is a series of principles to which courts must 'have regard' in making any financial decision on maintenance or property. The principles, summarised, are these:

1. The court must have regard to all the circumstances of the case, first consideration being given to the welfare of any child of the family under 18.

2. The court must in particular have regard to:

   - the income, earning capacity, property and other financial resources which the parties have or are likely to have

in the foreseeable future, including any increase in earning capacity which either party might reasonably acquire;
- the parties' financial needs, obligations and responsibilities – existing or foreseeable;
- the family's standard of living before the marriage broke down;
- the age of the parties and the duration of the marriage;
- any disability of either party;
- the contributions which the parties have made or are likely to make to the family's welfare, including contributions by way of looking after the home and family;
- the parties' conduct – if the court thinks it would be inequitable to disregard it.
- if the marriage is to be dissolved (in divorce and nullity cases) the value of pension benefits which either party will lose when they cease to be a spouse.

Some of these principles are brought into the picture when calculating gross and net income (see above). Others deal solely or mainly with problems of property and capital (see Chapter 15). But, as you will see, none has any firm figures attached.

How then can anyone – court, lawyer, or you and your partner – apply these principles to the hard facts of your existing financial position, and carve out of those hard facts equally hard decisions about maintenance?

The practical answer is that in the vast majority of cases the principles as such are ignored when the final carve-up is made. First time round, and save in the most extreme cases, courts and lawyers use long-established rules of thumb. And while on appeal higher courts may occasionally decide that one or other of the principles justifies some fine tuning of a first-time-round decision, the first-time-round decision is what holds in the vast majority of cases. All else apart, the cost of fighting any further invariably threatens all that any appeal might gain.

(b) The rules of thumb

Case A: Families of average income
Case A.1 Husband and wife with no children

For more than two centuries courts have considered that maintenance for a spouse who has no income should be one-third of the
income – net income, remember – of the other spouse. That principle
is still likely to be followed in such cases.

In modern times, when both spouses are likely to have income,
the courts have generally taken the view that no maintenance of
substance should be payable if the incomes of both are already
approximately equal.

Therefore, the extremes are reasonably well defined:

- One spouse produces all their joint income and the other none:
  the former pays one-third of joint income to the latter by way
  of maintenance.
- Each spouse produces approximately half of their joint income:
  neither pays maintenance to the other. But a court may still make
  a nominal maintenance order (say 5p a year) in favour of a
  spouse whose income is at risk – of redundancy, for example. A
  nominal order can later be increased if circumstances do change.

But where spouses' circumstances fall between those extremes (as
most do) court decisions and lawyers' views have been far more
variable.

How can you reasonably contain the results of that randomness,
and particularly the cost of fighting around it? The easiest answer is
for you and your partner first to work out:

- what your total joint net income is (add the two together)
- what percentage each of you contributes to that joint income
  (divide the figure for your separate incomes by the figure for
  joint income and multiply the result by 100 – or use a calculator).

Where do you go from there?

The courts have already set the extremes. You can normally
expect to end up with one-third (33 per cent) of joint income (by
way of maintenance) if your partner produces all the income. And
one-half (50 per cent) of joint income (by way of what you yourself
earn) if your incomes are equal. So your right to share in joint income
rises from one-third to one-half as your own contribution rises from
0 to 50 per cent.

You can define all positions in between logically simply by drawing a graph – Figure 14.1 overleaf is such a graph. And the line A–B

on Figure 14.1 suggests how your percentage share of joint income should rise (left-hand scale) as your percentage contribution to joint income does (bottom scale).

By using Figure 14.1 you can quickly discover how much of joint income you should have.

Suppose, for example, you contribute 40 per cent to joint income. Read along the bottom of Figure 14.1 to 40 per cent. Put a ruler straight up and mark the point on the line A–B above 40 per cent. Then use your ruler to find the point on the left-hand (vertical) scale which is opposite your mark and count off what percentage that is on the left hand scale (45 per cent if your income contributes 40 per cent).

That percentage defines logically what you should receive out of joint income.

And to calculate your maintenance?

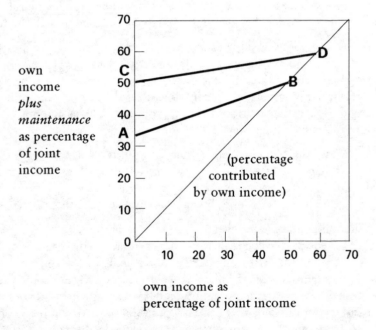

own income as
percentage of joint income

Note: A = 33%, B = 50% left-hand scale;
C = 50%, D = 58.5% left-hand scale.

Figure 14.1 *How to calculate your share of joint income*

- Work out what that percentage of joint income is (multiply joint income by the percentage figure).
- Deduct the amount of your own income from that figure.
- The amount of maintenance is what's left.

But bear in mind that there is nothing in law to justify this particular approach. Different figures might well emerge if you and your partner decided to let your separate lawyers battle it out – in or out of court. Even if they start with exactly the same figures, no two lawyers are ever likely to have exactly the same ideas about the way in which they should be carved up. On the other hand, Figure 14.1 is hardly capable of putting you in the wrong parish; it does no more than define stages between end positions which the courts have long adopted. And the costs you save by using Figure 14.1 are more than likely to balance any difference which argument might produce.

Case A.2 Husband and wife with children

Any Child Support payable for your own children should already have been decided by the Child Support Agency before any question arises of court maintenance for you; or for your partner; or for any stepchildren; or for any maintenance for your own children on top of Child Support.

The changes to your respective net incomes resulting from Child Support will already have been picked up in calculating net incomes under the principles discussed under 'Your incomes' above.

But if there is still a significant difference between your net incomes despite such adjustment, there may be a case for maintenance to be paid to reduce that difference. And in such cases maintenance in favour of the parent with care may extend beyond the point where parental incomes are equal.

How can this issue be approached?

The courts have always concentrated more on the resources available to family units as a whole than on those specific to individuals within those units. So when they have had to consider maintenance for a parent and children they have tended to calculate maintenance for the parent as in the case of husbands and wives alone (see A.1 above) and then add something on for the children.

But even when doing that they have recognised (as Child Support rules also do) that ordering anyone to pay more than half their income to support spouse and children is likely to invite default. So in a case where a parent with care had no income they would never be likely to order the absent parent to pay more than half (50 per cent) of his (or her) income to the parent with care and the children.

In such a case, therefore, one might find that the parent with care was awarded one-third (33 per cent) of the absent parent's income by maintenance – as would be the case if there were no children; and the children (ie if they were in their middle to late teens) a balance of 17 per cent at most.

But what if parents' incomes are already equal?

For the reasons already discussed there is then as such no case for maintenance to be paid between parents. But it is clearly not fair – or logical – that there should also be nothing for any dependent children. Legally, both parents are equally liable to maintain their children, and if both parents have equal incomes each should contribute in equal amounts.

Taken together these principles allow another logical and precise guideline for calculating maintenance where families with children are involved.

If 17 per cent of joint income is the maximum likely to be allowed for children on top of maintenance for a parent with care who has no income, half of that (8.5 per cent of joint income) is logically the maximum additional maintenance payable if parent with care and absent parent have equal incomes.

Using those two extremes it is possible to draw another logical line (the line C–D) on Figure 14.1. That line defines the *maximum* proportion of *joint* income which a parent with care and children should receive.

The maximum extra maintenance appropriate in such cases can be calculated in the same way as suggested for spouses without children by marking the vertical reference point on line C–D.

But bear in mind that it may only be appropriate to pay the whole of the maximum when children are in their teens. Only part of it may be required for younger or very young children.

Note:

- If this approach is followed, any case for 'extra' maintenance disappears once the income of the parent with care exceeds 60 per cent of the joint income. However, on the principles followed by the courts before the introduction of Child Support, that is probably appropriate.

- Any such 'extra' court maintenance is probably now best dealt with as maintenance for the parent with care – spouses who pay maintenance only qualify for limited tax allowances, but they only qualify for those in respect of maintenance paid to a former spouse who has not remarried.

- The courts have always had the power to order parents with care to pay maintenance to absent parents – and might still do that if a parent with care generates the large part of the parties' joint income, and particularly if the absent parent is disabled. But there is no comparable balance in the Child Support rules. If an absent parent has an assessable income under those rules, that parent is liable to pay Child Support however high the income of the parent with care may be. It is therefore possible that the courts may, in due course, reverse extreme consequences of the Child Support rules by ordering parents with care to pay maintenance to absent parents, despite the fact that Child Support is payable the other way.

Case B: Rich families

If the amount of maintenance calculated as suggested (or by any other means) is more than you or your partner need to maintain the standard of living you enjoyed while you were together – or could have enjoyed if one of you had not been excessively stingy – maintenance is likely to be limited to such amount as will keep you going as you were. If this is likely to be the case you will need a complete annual budget for the relevant partner to define the limit.

Case C: Poor families
Case C.1 Husband, Wife and no children

The lower your joint income becomes, the more likely a court is to order maintenance which leaves you with equal shares. If, for example, a husband has £120 a week net income and a wife has none, he may have to pay her £60 a week maintenance, not the £40 which the one-third principle would suggest.

As with everything else in the law governing family finances there is no line drawn which separates the poor, the average and the rich, and there seem to be nearly as many approaches to the grey areas as there are people making decisions on them. As a rough guide, you and your partner are likely to have to start thinking about poverty making some difference to the way your incomes may be carved up if your joint gross income is below the level of the average non-manual national wage – £18,174 in 1994.

The further you fall below that level the more likely you are to have to face an equal split of joint net income, whatever the proportions each of you contributes to it. But if both of you are receiving means-tested social security benefits – or have incomes at that level – a clean break may be appropriate (see Chapter 17).

Case C.2 Husband and wife with children

Child Support is likely to mop up everything available. It already includes substantial provision for parents with care (see Chapter 13, pages 91, 96 and 99), and parents with low incomes are unlikely to have any scope to pay more. A nominal order (say 5p a year) may be appropriate if there is a real possibility that circumstances may improve in the future. But otherwise a clean break may make sense (see Chapter 17, pages 134 and 136).

15

Rights to property, savings and investments: Married couples and all children

The legal background to property decisions

Only since 1970 have the courts had the power to rearrange spouses' property after divorce. So the principles applied in making property decisions are nothing like as fully developed as they are with maintenance, which has been around for more than 200 years.

When considering who shall have what the law merely directs the courts 'to have regard' to the same set of general principles as apply in maintenance cases. As these are summarised in detail in Chapter 14 (page 109–110) they are not repeated here. But as with maintenance there is no more detailed guidance.

Decided cases suggest that general principles have emerged for dealing with cases which involve short marriages, and spouses who are rich. They also suggest that if spouses of more modest means have been married for some time their assets are likely to be divided more or less equally between them if that is feasible.

But the cases also make it clear that if it is not practical or possible to sell, divide or share property owned by one spouse, and there is no other asset which can be used to compensate for its value, the other may end up with little or nothing of its value.

Thus, for example, if a wife has a business, a husband may not end up with any share in its value if that share can only be produced by selling the business and making those who work in it redundant. And if husband and wife own a house and have children, the partner who is to have care of the children may end up with the lion's share of the house if that is the only way to keep a roof over the children's heads.

As a result:

- Different principles may apply to different types of property.
- Although anything which spouses own may come into account and may in consequence have to be valued, there is no point in obtaining expensive valuations of any property owned by one spouse which is incapable of being shared (eg pension rights) unless that spouse has other property which can be transferred to compensate.

These principles are considered in greater detail in the sections which follow.

What property may be involved in sharing?

If a married couple separate (or children of any parents claim against either parent) *anything* they own may come into the reckoning. A court may in addition take account of any property which they might acquire – a likely inheritance, for example. If money or property is jointly owned their share will be treated as part of what they own.

Cash savings in a bank, a building society or other accounts have an obvious cash value. Other property such as houses, land, shares, pension rights and business interests may have to be valued. But (as the courts have made clear) there is no point in obtaining expensive valuations of property tied to one of you unless there are other free assets which can be transferred to the other to balance your shares.

So if: (a) your partner's interest in his or her pension scheme is all you have; and (b) under the scheme's rules no part of that can be transferred to you, nothing can be gained by knowing what that interest is worth. You can't receive a share in your partner's pension. And neither of you has anything else which you can receive instead.

Property – and its net value

Subject to that caution on valuations, before anyone can consider how your property ought to be shared you need to know:

1. Exactly what each of you owns – houses, furniture and contents, cars, businesses, land, shares, pension rights, life insurances, cash and other savings.
2. What your share is in anything you own jointly with others.
3. Whether you are likely to receive some asset in the foreseeable future – compensation for a pending accident claim or an inheritance, for example.
4. The net value, approximately at least, of 1., 2. and 3. above. Net value is what you would have left if:

   (a) everything which is not already in cash form, or calculable in cash terms, was sold up and added to the cash total;
   (b) all professional or other charges and taxes (eg Capital Gains Tax) payable following any such sale were paid;
   (c) all debts, mortgages and other liabilities (and your share of such liabilities on jointly owned property) were paid off.

Bear in mind that you are only individually liable for debts which you incurred in your own name, but that you and your partner are each liable (and usually each is liable for the full amount if the other does not pay) for debts incurred in *joint* names.

Once you each know the *net* value of the property you own, you will be able to see if there is any great difference between your existing positions. If there is, there may be a case for the one with more to transfer something to the one with less. But that case may depend on how all or any of the sections of this chapter which follow apply to your particular circumstances.

How might you share what you have?

Short marriages

Short marriage principles are likely to apply if you and your partner: (a) are relatively young; and (b) do not have any children; and (c) have only been married for a short time, say, two to three years or less (but if you lived together before marriage that period may be treated as part of your marriage).

In such cases courts are not likely to order partners to share any property or savings which they owned before they came together, or received as a gift or by inheritance from their own families. If the partner with less is still of an age to make his or her own fortune in life, marriage on its own is not usually considered a sufficient reason for making one partner richer at the expense of the other, or the family of the other.

But:

(a) Even short marriage partners are likely to have to share property which they put together jointly during their relationship – probably equally.

(b) If you are older, and one of you has assets and the other does not, the shortness of your marriage is not likely to make any difference. Comfortably established divorcees, widows and widowers, and people contemplating first marriages late in life should therefore think hard before marrying someone of comparable age who has very little.

(c) The shortness of a marriage is not likely to make any difference if you have children, since those children also have to be considered. Absent parents with assets are always likely to have to part with something to parents with care who have less, regardless of the length of their marriage.

Marriages not affected by short marriage principles – rich spouses

As in the case of maintenance:

(a) Spouses' previous standard of living is relevant if between them they have enough to allow both to go on living at the same standard after they separate, ie they are seriously rich.

(b) Any transfer of property or other assets is not likely to involve more than is needed to preserve the standard of living of the spouse to whom it is transferred.

Nevertheless, the message from two cases where spouses had been married for some years and were seriously rich (assets of £2 million or more) is that the 'poorer' spouse is likely to end up with about one-third of their joint assets – as long as assets sufficient to achieve that balance can readily be transferred or realised.

Marriages not affected by short marriage principles – spouses who are not rich

No children and all assets easily transferable

Broad equality is likely to be the guiding principle. So if your shares are already approximately equal you leave things more or less as they are. If not, you aim for equality: the partner with more transfers cash or property to the one with less. But either way it may still be practical for you to swap assets, particularly shares in jointly owned assets. If, for example, a house and a business are both jointly owned it may make sense for one of you to end up with the house and the other the business.

Assets not easily transferable and/or families with dependent children

In these cases it is rarely possible to achieve equality – or obvious fairness – because property cannot be or should not be sold, transferred or shared. And what you and your partner may reasonably be able to expect out of your joint property is therefore likely to depend entirely on its nature – the *type* of property involved.

So we shall look at the problem from that point of view:

The contents of the family home

If you own works of art or antiques with a substantial resale value they can be professionally valued or, of course, sold. Such items can therefore reasonably be treated as if they are cash and their value can be brought into account as available cash (see 'Free cash' below).

But most of what people have in their homes ('residual goods') cost a great deal more than it is ever likely to realise if sold, although it might cost at least as much as it originally did to replace it. And most of the cash value of your residual goods is likely to be swallowed up if you pay to have them valued, fight about them in court, or send them to auction.

So the only sensible answer with residual goods is for you and your partner to keep them, and agree how to share them out between you. The following suggestions may help you to do that:

(a) Goods subject to hire purchase, conditional sale, rental or other agreements not fully paid. These will continue to be the legal liability of whoever signed the agreement – both of you if both did (don't

forget any items hired or rented from gas, electricity or telephone companies). Remember, it is usually a condition of such agreements that the goods shall be kept at the address shown in the agreement, and there may be penalties if you cancel any such agreement. So if that is what you plan to do read the small print (and perhaps take legal advice) before contacting any finance company. Otherwise:

- If your partner is going to keep goods which you have signed for in your own name, or jointly, the finance company may agree to transfer the agreement into your partner's name. But otherwise you will have to work out who is to pay for them between you – you will still be legally liable if the finance company is not paid.
- In any event, inform the finance company if the goods are to be moved to a different address.

(b) Children and residual goods. Children's interests always come first. If you have children they are likely to go on needing everything you and your partner have bought them, or have used regularly to provide for them, or which is required to maintain their home. And none of it is likely to be worth much by the time they have finished with it. So that part of your residual goods ought to stay with the parent with care – even if that means most of what you both have as it often does.

(c) The rest of your residual goods. These are best divided like this:

1. Each of you should keep your own clothes and other entirely personal items, *plus* anything you owned before you and your partner came together, *plus* anything given to you personally by your own family or friends.
2. Each of you should keep gifts you have received from your partner. But if they are valuable their cash value ought to be included in your free cash calculations (see below); valuable jewellery is an example.
3. Each of you should keep any tools or equipment you use for your job and any equipment which you alone use (a sewing machine, for example).
4. A car or (cars) should stay with the spouse who most regularly uses/needs it (for work, for example) but it should be valued and its value should be included in the free cash calculations (see below).

5. Each of you should pay any outstanding debts specifically incurred in connection with any of the items listed in 1.–4. above
   without contribution from the other.
6. The rest of your belongings ought to be divided more or less equally
   (in value) between you. That may be easier said than done but:

   - If you own sets or several similar items of the same thing
     (cutlery, crockery or bed linen, for examples) these are
     fairly easy to split.
   - If one of you wants to keep one particular item (perhaps
     a chair) and the other another (perhaps a table) try to
     agree swaps.
   - If all else fails you might still solve your problem without
     the ruinous cost of a court battle by using an old approach.
     Under ancient British law it was the wife's job to divide the
     household goods into two equal piles, and the husband had
     first choice of pile. Frankly, there is no modern approach
     to this particular problem which matches the economy,
     subtlety or sophistication of that solution.

Free cash
The term 'free cash' is here used to include:

(a) Cash which you or your partner have at home or have saved in
    bank, building society, post office or other accounts, premium
    bonds or other fixed value holdings.
(b) The cash value of significant residual goods – cars, works of art,
    antiques, jewellery (see above) – even if one of you wishes or
    intends to keep the item.
(c) The current cash value of stocks, shares, unit trust holdings and
    similar investments (usually listed in broadsheet newspapers)
    and of any variable National Savings investments (eg Index
    Linked Bonds – National Savings will advise values); surrender
    values of endowment insurances (insurance companies will ad-
    vise – although policies nearing maturity may sometimes be sold
    for more); any other investment of comparable nature.

If you and your partner own no more than the contents of your home
and free cash, that is all either of you have to pay off any existing
debts and liabilities. Each of you on your own should carry any
liability incurred through buying any particular item you are to keep

individually. But the total of any other debts outstanding should come out of the total of your free cash.

Once you have the figures you should aim to divide the total of your free cash equally between you, using cash actually available (in savings accounts, and so on) to balance any value each receives by retaining valuable items in kind. If you earn more than your partner, you may well feel that you have contributed more to your savings, and so should have more out of them. But while different principles may apply to other property such as houses (see 'Flats and houses' below), these days the courts tend to take the view that, in the average family, husbands and wives contribute equal value to contents and savings. As a judge put it years ago 'The cock can only feather the nest because the hen is sitting on it.'

Here is an example of how free cash might be calculated.

Husband (H) has a car worth £2,500; shares valued at £1,000; an endowment policy with £500 surrender value; and debts of £600 still to pay on gas, electricity and telephone accounts. Wife (W) has a car worth £500, £100 Premium Bonds, a ring worth £250, and a debt of £200 still to pay for groceries bought on her bank card. They have £2,500 in a joint building society account, out of which they would normally have drawn money to pay the larger household bills. Each wants to keep the cars, shares etc they have in their own names, but they may change their minds when they work out the figures.

These are their separate positions:

	H	W
Car	£2,500	£500
Shares	£1,000	–
Endowment policy	£500	–
Premium Bonds	–	100
Ring	–	250
Half building society A/C	1,250	1,250
Total	5,250	2,100
Less debts	600	200
Net	4,650	1,900

Jointly, therefore, they have net £4,650 (H) + £1,900 (W) = £6,550, and half of that is £3,275. So H must pay W £1,375 if they are to end up equal. In other words, W has all the Building Society money plus £125.

But bear in mind:

(a) Such an equal approach may only be appropriate if spouses have contents and free cash to consider.

(b) If there were additional assets a court might award more of the cash to a partner who ended up with less of the other assets.

Flats and houses
(a) Rented accommodation

- If you *both* intend to give up your accommodation – or you have to because neither will any longer be able to afford it – first check any lease or tenancy agreement to find out how, when or if you can end it, and what ending it may cost you.

- If only *one* of you wants to keep your accommodation your landlord will probably agree to transfer the tenancy into the name of that one alone, if that is not already how things stand. And a court may order such a transfer by consent in any event. But local authority and housing association landlords may reconsider whether one of you alone still satisfies their housing need priorities and *might* end the tenancy if you do not.

- If *both* of you want to keep your accommodation:

  - Children (and so parents with care in married couples) have first claim. In disputed cases courts are likely to order tenancy transfers in their favour; and local authorities and housing associations may transfer tenancies by administrative action.

  - If you do not have dependent children courts, local authorities and housing associations are likely to favour the spouse with the greater need – the one less likely to be able to find any alternative.

You and your partner will save legal costs if you can agree which of you is to have any rented flat or house in the light of these principles.

(b) Owner-occupied accommodation
- If you *both* intend to sell your accommodation – or you have to because neither will any longer be able to afford it – try to agree

how you will sell it (eg the estate agents/solicitors you will use) and how you will look after and pay for the property until it can be sold.

- If *one* of you is to stay on in the property until the sale it is usually reasonable that that one should pay running costs until the sale. If the property is to stand empty it is usually reasonable that each of you should contribute to ongoing expenses in the same proportion as you agree to share the ultimate proceeds of sale. But the outstanding amount of any mortgage and any estate agent and legal charges incurred on the sale will also have to come out of the proceeds.
- How should you share what's left? Normally equally.
- If *either* of you wants to keep your accommodation (and as long as you can afford it once your means are divided):

  - If your house is so valuable that both of you (and/or any children in the care of one of you) would be able to buy suitable alternative accommodation if it was sold and the proceeds of sale divided between you, sale and division of the proceeds is what a court is nevertheless likely to order if you cannot agree.
  - Otherwise, again children come first. A court is likely to allow the parent with care to stay on in the home if you cannot agree. And a court might also so decide in favour of children of an unmarried couple. But the right of the parent with care/children to stay on is likely to end when the youngest child reaches the age of 17. Typically, a court will order that then: the house shall be sold, and the net proceeds of the sale divided between married parents, or paid to whichever unmarried parent is legal owner – both if they are joint owners.

In cases involving unmarried parents any ultimate sharing will depend on the rules which govern property rights (see Chapter 16).

In cases involving married parents, parents with care who stay on in the home are likely to get more than half of the ultimate net proceeds – perhaps 60 to 75 per cent in an average case; and perhaps 80 per cent up to 100 per cent if the other parent has or can easily acquire secure alternative accommodation; or has a new partner who is rich and able to look after him or her.

These differences arise because parents with care have to start from scratch when their houses are sold or if they later buy out the interest of the other parent (which such arrangements usually allow); and the longer the delay the harder that may be. And by then absent parents have *had* to find alternatives, however easy or difficult that may have been.

A final point: you need to consider who is to maintain and insure any accommodation in which one of you is to remain for some time after you separate, and who is to pay any mortgage and other ongoing expenses until sale.

If no children are involved, your ages, the length of your marriage, and the fact that one of you may have greater difficulty in finding somewhere else to live are likely to be what matter.

(a) Once spouses pass their mid-forties courts may well allow which-ever of them is likely to have greater difficulty in finding another home to stay on in the matrimonial home. They may order that the house be transferred to the needy spouse completely. But more often that spouse will be given limited rights which end:

- if the spouse remarries, lives with someone else as if married, or ceases to use the house as his or her main home; or
- after a fixed period if the spouse ought to be able to find an alternative in the time fixed; or
- when the relevant spouse dies.

The first of these three options is the most common.

When any such limited residential right ends, courts will usually order that the property shall be sold and the net proceeds shared between the spouses – as where sale is delayed in the children's interest. But in such cases they are more likely to order an equal split of the proceeds, unless the one who is to stay on will in the mean time have to pay off a substantial part of the amount borrowed on any mortgage or similar debt.

(b) If younger couples cannot agree, immediate sale and division of the net proceeds (usually equally) is the most likely outcome.

Family businesses

If both of you have been involved in running a family business and have each been looking after different activities which can stand alone, splitting the business so you each have your own may be the answer. Sometimes couples who have run businesses together find that they can still work together, even though they cannot live together.

But usually one partner is the main mover in family businesses; whoever has the business will have to keep it if the business is to survive; and all their partner can expect out of it is likely to be limited to whatever can reasonably be raised by borrowing or by drawing out any uninvested cash.

Often that bears little or no relationship to the business's value. So in a case where a husband had worked for 20 years to build up a semi-derelict farm which his wife's father had originally given them, the wife and their children kept the farm which by then was worth £110,000. He received only £15,000. That was all the wife could reasonably raise by borrowing without having to sell up.

If you or your partner have a business, you may well need help from an accountant to work out what can be done. But if you hope to agree, remember that the courts are never likely to order anything which will destroy a business and the jobs which go with it, or which will make it impossible for the spouse who is running it to go on earning enough to pay maintenance.

Pension rights

Pension rights have a value and they can be valued. But the spouse who has the pension rights usually has to keep them – they cannot normally be divided between spouses after divorce. If you and your partner have other property, it may be possible to balance the value of the pension rights which one of you has by giving extra (out of the rest of your property) to the other. If that is possible it is what you should aim for. But if there is no extra there is nothing either of you can do about it.

Completing your arrangements

You will save yourselves the main part of any likely legal costs if you can agree between you all the details of what you have, what it is worth and how it is to be shared. But your agreement will not be final and binding unless it is spelled out in a court order. And you may need legally effective documents (to deal with property transfers or new mortgage arrangements, for example) to put your agreement into effect. So even if you reach full agreement a solicitor who regularly deals with such problems is still likely to be helpful in getting the paperwork right.

If you cannot agree you will have to fight it out between you, probably each with separate solicitors; and, if they cannot produce an agreement acceptable to you both, in court. A court order will be the end result of that approach too. But the cost of getting it will swallow a substantial slice of all you own – reported costs figures in such cases frequently run into tens of thousands of pounds.

16

Rights to property, savings and investments: Unmarried couples

Rights defined in advance

English law will not enforce marriage contracts. If married couples separate the courts can rearrange anything they have previously agreed. But the courts do enforce similar agreements made between unmarried couples. Such agreements may relate to particular property – a house, for example; or they may cover all the property which the partners have.

If they relate to particular property the agreement is likely to be spelled out in the deeds or documents of title of that property. But any such agreement must be in writing, and for technical legal reasons should be spelled out in a formal deed.

If you and your partner have so defined your property shares in advance, those shares are what you will get if you split up.

Rights not previously defined

This is how legal rights are likely to stand if you have not previously defined them:

Property not in joint names

(a) You will each be legally entitled to keep anything you owned before you came together, which was given to you personally (lifetime gift or inheritance) by relations or friends, or which you received or are entitled to receive exclusively in your own right; eg compensation for dismissal, redundancy or injury, pensions from your own employment, awards or prizes which you have received or won.

(b) You will each be entitled to keep anything bought exclusively with your own money – even if bought in the name of your partner. But if your partner has in fact contributed cash or its equivalent to property which is in your name, your partner may have a right to a share of it. For example:

- your partner has worked with you to build or convert a house;
- your partner's wage has gone into your joint household expenses so that it has been easier for you to pay for some things because your partner was paying for others (see 'Common fund purchases' below).

Property and savings in joint names

(a) If either of you can draw on savings accounts without the signature of the other, or the deeds of your house or any other land say that you own it as joint tenants, the survivor will take the lot if one of you dies. If you separate you can (and should) end that risk by freezing joint accounts (written notice to the account holder), and by serving *written* notice (notice of severance – see Chapter 9, pages 56–58) on your partner to end a *joint* tenancy of landed property. But after that has been done you will be entitled to share the property *equally*.

(b) If both of you have to sign to draw on joint savings accounts, or the deeds of your house or land say that you own it as tenants in common without any definition of your shares, there will be a basic assumption that you are entitled to share these equally. But if you can prove that you have contributed cash or its value in unequal shares (see 'Common fund purchases' below), the proportions in which you have contributed will decide your shares.

Common fund purchases

(a) If you have both contributed earnings or savings to your household while you were together, you will each have a right to share

in anything which you have then bought either jointly or separately.
If you can prove the proportions in which you have contributed,
your shares will be broadly in those proportions, but otherwise
equal rights may be assumed. That said, it's not usually sensible or
practical to argue differences over individual household items. But
you can use the same principles as married couples for dividing up
your household goods (see Chapter 15, page 121–122).

(b) If you have contributed cash value to property which you have
acquired since you came together you are entitled to a reasonable
share in that property. A classic example came with a case where
a man and his fiancée worked together to build a house. She ran
the cement mixer and did other building work alongside him.
The courts decided that she was entitled to one-third of its value
when they later split up. But your contribution has to be
something of that nature. Ordinary work round the house – even
painting, decorating and other maintenance – gets you nowhere.
Even after 19 years together a woman qualified for nothing
because she had merely kept her man's house and brought up
their children.

Overriding issues

Remember that:

1. The courts can still intervene to change the property rights of
   either of you if you have children and their interest requires it
   (see Chapter 11, page 73 and Chapter 15, page 118).
2. If your partner dies while you are still living together you may
   have a claim for reasonable provision for your maintenance out
   of your partner's estate, regardless of who might otherwise be
   entitled to what – see Chapter 19).

Solicitors and costs

If you can agree who shall have what by applying these principles you
may still need a solicitor's help to sort out the paperwork, particularly
if houses or land are involved. But as with the married you will save
yourselves a small fortune in costs if you can agree the detail.

17

Divorce and the clean break

What is a clean break?

Following divorce or nullity, courts must by law consider if circumstances are such that:

1. no maintenance should be paid; or
2. maintenance should be limited to a period sufficient to allow the maintained spouse to adjust to independent living without undue hardship.

If they decide that there should be a time limit on, or no, maintenance, the order they make to record their decision is known as a clean break order.

Married couples may agree that neither of them shall have any right to ongoing maintenance and courts may sometimes make a clean break order even if they do not agree. But in every case:

(a) There has to be a court order to make the clean break legally effective (such orders usually also wrap up any future right to claim maintenance out of the estate of a deceased partner – see Chapter 19, page 149).

(b) No clean break order can limit or exclude children's rights to ongoing maintenance or the powers of the Child Support Agency – see Chapter 13).

Why is a clean break desirable?

You have to make a new start if your marriage dies. Maintenance makes that difficult whether you pay or receive it. Neither of you can be truly independent while one still depends on the other. And maintenance often becomes a running sore, poisoning what is left of the regard which former spouses had for each other, and contaminating relationships which they have with any children.

Nor can you rely on maintenance. The courts can always change the amount if the financial circumstances of either of you change. It may be difficult (sometimes impossible) to squeeze maintenance out of a former partner who fails to pay, or fails to pay regularly. And if you have to claim means-tested social security benefits – anyway or because maintenance is not coming through – those payments will still be affected by any right to maintenance. The DSS reduces such social security benefits to allow for any maintenance payable. If maintenance is not paid some time may elapse before the DSS makes your money up. And if you finally recover arrears of maintenance, DSS support will be reduced to allow for them.

So your future is far more predictable if ongoing maintenance does not feature in it. And because of the social security aspect that may be true even if you end up with little to show for a clean break deal – merely your household goods, for example.

When clean breaks make sense

When you/your partner are rich enough to compensate for no maintenance – in whole or part

You will each be entitled to your appropriate share of your family's property and assets under the principles discussed in Chapter 15. You will also be entitled to (or have to pay) Child Support, and perhaps maintenance on top, if you have children; and the younger they are the longer that will go on. So the most that any clean break deal can cover is any maintenance which would be payable between you.

You can make a reasonable estimate of that maintenance by following the principles set out in Chapter 14. But when calculating net incomes for a clean break maintenance calculation, you do not deduct superannuation or pension payments (Chapter 14, page 108). If there is not to be any ongoing maintenance the benefit of such payments will go to the partner who makes them – that benefit will not feature in future calculations of income and maintenance. So such payments do not figure in clean break maintenance calculations.

Once you have maintenance figures you need to consider how long maintenance might otherwise be payable.

The basic purpose of maintenance is to tide the maintained partner over until that partner can reasonably be expected to adjust to independence (see page 133). Scottish law puts a figure of three years on that for average cases. But in real life age, fitness, qualifications, work experience, the age of dependent children, or the length of the marriage may all affect an individual's chances of getting back on his or her own feet. A recently married couple who both still have the jobs they had before marriage may not need any time to adjust. A fit young parent with small children may well be capable of restoring full earning power once all children reach secondary school age at the latest. But a spouse well on in middle age who married young and has not been employed since may never be able to.

Other factors also enter into estimates of the duration of maintenance. Maintenance ends with the remarriage or death of the partner entitled to it, and *on average* adult maintenance is not paid for more than eight years. Therefore, reckoning a period between three and eight years is not usually likely to be far from the mark unless some particular aspect of your circumstances makes it clear that that will not be enough.

Multiply your maintenance figure by the number of years it is likely to be paid and you have a rough idea of the total likely to be involved over that period. But if a partner liable to maintenance is to pay something extra to the other (ie on top of his or her normal property share) for an immediate clean break, even that figure should be reduced to allow for early payment.

Rich people can usually find enough to finance full compensation for the ending of maintenance with a clean break – and they can also afford the often vast cost of paying skilled professionals to argue, and work out, detailed figures for them. But most of us are not rich, cannot afford that expense, and may at most only be able to compensate in part.

Nevertheless, a clean break may still make sense, even if all you get out of it is a greater share in your house (maybe all of it) or in some other asset which would otherwise be shared between you and your partner. No one can know the future. A bird in your hand now will usually be a far better bet than any chance in the lottery of future maintenance.

Even if neither of you has all that much, both of you are still likely to end up better off if you can agree a clean break deal which nevertheless makes sense to you. Since the law offers no precise legal guidelines about rights and liabilities, common sense should never be despised. And, even allowing for the fact that you may still need lawyers' skills to get a clean break order right, your own common sense clean break deal will come a lot cheaper than employing professionals to fight your way to one.

When you/your partner are not rich enough to pay any significant compensation in place of maintenance

A clean break deal and order may still make sense even if all that one of you gets out of it is the contents of your home; or even if both of you are stony-broke and are likely to stay that way. Always remember:

(a) If either or both of you have to rely on means-tested social security benefits a clean break will prevent any chance of maintenance complicating benefit claims and payments – although, of course, nothing will change your rights to, or liabilities for, Child Support.

(b) As long as the right to maintenance stays alive either of you can come back against the other (or his or her estate) for maintenance at any time in the future unless he or she has remarried. So too can the DSS (under liable relative rules) if either of you later claims means-tested benefits, and the other has in the mean time become a little better off.

(c) The right to claim maintenance cuts both ways – former wives may claim against former husbands but former husbands may also claim against former wives. And the fact that one of you may be better off now does not mean that those positions may not reverse in future. You may both be better off without that risk hanging over you.

When clean breaks may not make sense

There may be no sense in agreeing a clean break if:

1. one of you has, or is likely to have, a sizeable income; and

2. the other has little or no income and no real prospect of having one; and
3. neither of you has any property or assets of substance which can compensate for abandoning the right to maintenance.

What do the courts do with clean breaks?

The courts will usually make a clean break order by consent whenever the parties agree and whatever their financial circumstances. But they have proved far less willing to impose such orders in the absence of agreement except when the deal includes substantial compensation for the ending of maintenance.

18

Children: Their care – and parental responsibility

Earlier chapters dealt with financial rights and duties if you have children. This chapter looks at other rights and duties; at the arrangements and court orders which you should try to agree if you separate; and the decisions which a court may reach if you do not agree.

Parental responsibility

A practical definition of parental responsibility is that it wraps up all the rights and duties which married parents have with regard to their children while they are living happily together. Parental responsibility includes the right to name a person to act as a child's guardian if the parent should die.

Mothers always have parental responsibility for their children. So do fathers if married to mothers when their children were born.

If parents are not married fathers can acquire parental responsibility if both parents sign an agreement in form laid down by regulations; or by applying to the court for a parental responsibility order.

But anyone who has care of a child may do anything necessary to safeguard its interests regardless of parental responsibility. And a man does not have to have parental responsibility before he becomes legally liable to maintain his child. That liability exists as soon as he admits that he is its father, or his paternity is proved in court if he denies it. These days the courts can order that father and child provide samples for genetic fingerprinting which is almost universally conclusive as to whether or not a man is a child's father.

Basically, any parent with parental responsibility may exercise any right with regard to his or her child, which parents usually exercise, unless a court has made an order which limits that right. But even then a parent may only exercise such right to the extent that the other parent agrees – actually or by implication. So it may still be a criminal offence for a parent to take a child out of the care of the other without the other's agreement. If that should happen the parent with actual care should immediately inform the police who can take immediate action under the Child Abduction Acts.

If parents separate, their respective parental rights will be limited to those consistent with any Residence, Contact, Prohibited Steps or Specific Issues orders which a court may then make (see below).

Residence orders

If you separate, your children may still want to live with both of you. But the courts take the view that children should have a single definite home; and they are not likely to agree to any half-and-half or other arrangement unless that is the way the children and both parents want it.

If only one of you will be able to look after the children (and wants to) you should agree Residence in favour of that one – that's the best that you or the courts can do for them.

If both of you (or perhaps some other member of your families) could and are willing to look after the children you have to consider what – objectively and at the time – is in their best interest. That is what the law requires and that is all the courts will consider if you cannot agree. But the courts are nevertheless likely to accept any arrangement agreed by all of you – and 'all' may include the children themselves if they are old and mature enough to have a reliable view.

But bear in mind that if a court has to decide it is likely to follow the following principles:

1. If the children have been in the sole care of either parent for a lengthy period it is best for them to stay with that parent.
2. In any other case:

    (a) young children are best left with their mother – and they are likely to be considered young at least until they finish at primary school;

(b) female children are best left with their mothers whatever their age;

(c) children are best kept together.

3. Any views the children have themselves should only enter into the matter if they are of an age and maturity to understand what is involved.

For these and also for practical reasons most children stay or end up with their mothers. In the absence of agreement fathers are only likely to be granted Residence orders in extreme cases. For example:

- where a mother was proved to be mentally unstable and obsessed with a religious sect;
- where a 12-year-old girl refused to live with her mother under any circumstances.

Contact orders

For the reasons discussed in Chapter 5 most children need the fullest possible continuing contact with their 'absent' parent after separation. But normally the courts will make a Contact order without more – expecting you and your partner to agree reasonable arrangements and to stand by them.

Contact orders are usually made in court proceedings between the parents. But a child can also apply to the court for contact with either parent. Thus a boy who had lost touch with his father and wanted to trace him has used such an application to obtain details of his father's whereabouts from the Child Support Agency.

If a 'resident' parent makes continued contact difficult, a court may spell out days and times and order that contact be supervised by a child welfare officer. In an extreme case it might decide that obstacles to contact prove that the wrong parent was given a Residence order – and reverse the Residence order in favour of the other parent. And in theory (though hardly ever in practice) a court could commit an offending parent to prison for contempt of court.

Generally, contact is only ever likely to be refused altogether if a court is satisfied that continued contact will expose a child to real danger.

Grandparents may also apply to a court for a Contact order unless the grandchild is in local authority care (see below). But such an order will only be granted if the court is satisfied that it is in the interest of the grandchild. Normally, that will only be the case if the grandchild already has a good and well-developed relationship with the grandparents; or if the grandparent's own child – parent of the grandchild – has died, or disappeared, or is unable to maintain contact with the child for some other reason.

Specific Issues orders

Such orders are rare. If made, they deal with things which should be done in a child's interest – arranging for medical treatment if parents will not arrange it, for example.

Prohibited Steps orders

These orders are also rare. If made, they deal with things which should not be done – take a child abroad, for example.

Adoption

Adoption by unmarried adults

In times past unmarried mothers adopted their own children to hide the fact that their children had been conceived outside marriage. Single mothers may still adopt their own children – and possibly single fathers of an otherwise abandoned child. But this is the only case in which unmarried people may adopt and such adoptions are now rare. The stigma of illegitimacy has gone, all children are legally equal, and all adopted children now have the right to obtain copies of their original birth certificate once they are 18.

Adoption by married adults

Otherwise only married couples may adopt. But even then the interest of the child – and particularly its need, wherever possible, to know and preserve its true identity – remains the law's overriding concern. So married natural parents and step-parents will not normally be allowed to adopt children of the natural parent. And grandparents with an established relationship with such a child have successfully applied to the court for cancellation of an Adoption order made in such a case.

Local authority care

Local councils have a legal duty to provide full-time care for any child whose welfare requires it. Any child received into local authority care will be placed with suitable foster parents if available, and otherwise in a local authority home.

Local authority care may be entirely voluntary. Any parent not able to look after a child (even if only for a short period – while in hospital, for example) may ask his or her local authority to stand in.

But if voluntary care continues for some time the child's need for stability may begin to weigh against the parent's wish to have the child back. A local authority may then apply to the court for a Compulsory Care order, or established foster parents for a Residence order.

If a police officer considers that a child is at risk of real harm he can immediately remove it to a suitable place and place it under police protection. Anyone can apply to a Magistrates Family Proceedings Court for an order that a child be removed to a place of safety. But these are emergency measures and a child so removed cannot then be held for more than eight days unless the local authority starts full-scale Compulsory Care proceedings within that time.

Local councils will only be granted full-scale Compulsory Care orders if a court is satisfied that a child is suffering (or is likely to suffer) real harm through the absence of reasonable parental care; or because the child is out of parental control.

But if a Compulsory Care (or foster parent Residence) order is made, and is not reversed on appeal, the local authority takes over all parental responsibility and no one else has any rights over the child except such as the local authority may then agree.

Wardship

An application to make a child a ward of court may only be made to the Family Division of the High Court. A child becomes a ward as soon as the application is made and remains so unless or until the order is discharged. As long as wardship continues the court has exclusive command of every aspect of the child's life.

But virtually every normal aspect of child welfare is now covered by the powers of the Magistrates Courts to make Residence, Contact, Specific Issues, Prohibited Steps and Local Authority Care orders; and by the powers of the police under the Child Abduction Acts. And the courts will refuse wardship applications when any other remedy suffices. So a child is now only ever likely to become a ward of court if there are problems which Magistrates Courts cannot deal with – as there may be, for example, if a child owns substantial property.

19

Inheritance and wills

Wills, intestacy and statutory rights

If your partner features in your will – as executor, guardian of your children or beneficiary – he or she will continue to have any role or advantage given by your will until you make a new one; or, if you don't and are married, until the grant of Decree Absolute in divorce or nullity.

If you are married but have *not* made a will, your partner will continue to be entitled to the lion's share of your property under the laws which then apply (the Intestacy Rules – see below) until Decree Absolute. But unmarried couples have no rights under these rules.

If you separate, wills or a new will may be the last thing you want to think about. But if you own anything of value, or may acquire something of value in the future (by inheritance if a relative or friend dies, for example), you should consider making a will as soon as possible.

Even if you make a will, or leave the intestacy rules to sort things out, your property may not automatically end up with the beneficiaries named in your will or identified by those rules. In certain circumstances others close to you (including your former partner) may still have a claim on your estate under the Inheritance (Provision for Family and Dependants) Act 1975 (see 'Claims under the 1975 Inheritance Act' below).

But by making a will you will give those you name as beneficiaries the best chance of receiving what you want them to.

Making a will

You do not have to employ a solicitor to make your will, though any solicitor can do this for you if you wish. But you must observe basic legal rules meticulously if you are to get it right yourself; and you will be wise also to follow some common-sense principles:

These are the musts and the common sense principles:

Writing your will

1. A will must be in writing. Don't leave gaps in the text; and don't alter anything after the will has been signed (see below).
2. It is safer if your will says that any previous will is revoked.
3. It saves future cost if your will names your executors. These are the people who have the legal duty to collect your estate, pay your liabilities, and distribute what's left as your will directs. Any reliable person over 18 (including someone who is to benefit under your will) may be an executor.
4. Your will must name the people you wish to benefit and it should spell out what they are to have as simply as possible. Get a solicitor if you want to do complicated things.
5. Your will must carry the date when you sign it.
6. You save future costs if your will includes special words at the end which certify that the will has been properly signed and witnessed (see the example below).

To sign your will

1. You need two witnesses. Your witnesses must not be named as beneficiaries of your estate under 4. above, or be husband or wife of such a person, or they will lose the gift you intend them to have. But otherwise any reliable person over 18 will do.
2. You must sign the will at the end in the presence of both witnesses, both witnesses must then also sign (it helps if they add their addresses and occupations), and all three of you must stay together until you have all signed – so that each sees the others sign. If you have altered anything in your will before signing you should each initial any alteration when you sign.

You can buy will forms with printed instructions from stationers.

But you can also write your will on any suitable sheet of paper. If you follow the example below, you should, of course, write your own details in place of those shown in brackets. You should leave out Clause 3 and renumber the clause which follows if you do not have children under 18 – or do not wish to name a guardian.

Example

THIS WILL is made by me [Mary Smith] of [44 Long Street Sandbach] in the [County of Cheshire]

1. I REVOKE all former wills made by me.
2. I APPOINT [my brother John Smith] of [21 New Close Islington in the City of London] and [my sister Clare Johnson] of [14 High Street Newport Isle of Wight] to be the EXECUTORS and TRUSTEES of this will.
3. I APPOINT [my sister the said Clare Johnson] to be GUARDIAN of my children [Peter Michael Smith and Annie Joan Smith] until they reach the age of 18.
4. I GIVE all my estate to [my two children Peter Michael Smith and Annie Joan Smith] in [equal shares].

IN WITNESS WHEREOF I have hereunto set my hand this [21st] day of [February] 19[95]

SIGNED by the said [Mary Smith] in our presence and attested by us in the presence of [her] and each other } [Mary Smith's signature]

[Graham Blake's witness signature, 12 West Street, Sandbach, Cheshire.]

[Mechanic]

[June Thomas' witness signature, 42 Long Street, Sandbach, Cheshire.]

[Housewife]

If you get all the details right your will is effective as soon as it is signed. It is then an important legal document and should be kept in a safe place. Make sure that others – your executors, for example – also have photocopies or other true copies of the finished document. If the original is lost or accidentally destroyed a copy may do in its place. But remember that you cancel your will if you destroy it deliberately, intending to cancel it.

The intestacy rules

This is what happens to your property if you die without making a will:

1. If you are still legally married (ie before Decree Absolute) when you die:

    (a) Your partner takes everything if you have no children or descendants of children (eg grandchildren), no surviving parent, and no brothers or sisters of the whole blood (ie you have both parents in common) or descendants of such brothers or sisters.

    (b) If you have no children or descendants of children but do have any of the other relatives listed in (a) above, your partner takes your personal property in your house plus the first £200,000 of your estate plus the income for life from half of the remainder. Your other relatives qualify for what's left.

    (c) If you have children, your partner takes your personal property plus the first £125,000 of your estate plus the income for life from half the remainder. Your children take the other half immediately and the remainder when your partner dies.

    So you have to be quite well off before anyone except your former partner gets anything if you are still legally married. Make a will immediately if you do not want that to happen.

2. If you are not legally married when you die:

(a) Your children share everything equally – grandchildren etc share equally the share of any child of yours who died before you.

(b) If you have no one in category (a) above but your parents survive you they take everything – equally if both survive, so think carefully if they have separated.

(c) If you have no one in categories (a) or (b) above but do have brothers or sisters of the whole blood who survive you they take everything equally – their descendants also qualify for the share of any parent who died before you.

(d) If you have no one in categories (a), (b) or (c) above but are survived by half-brothers or sisters they take everything – their descendants also qualify for the share of any parent who died before you.

(e) If you have no one in categories (a), (b), (c) or (d) above but are survived by grandparents they take everything – equally if both survive, so again think carefully if they have separated.

(f) If you have no one in any of the previous categories but do have aunts or uncles of the whole blood who survive you they take everything equally – their descendants also qualify for the share of any parent who died before you.

(g) If you have no one in any of the previous categories but do have aunts or uncles of the half blood who survive you they take everything equally – their descendants also qualify for the share of any parent who died before you.

(h) If you have no one in any of the previous categories the Crown takes everything. Someone close to you (including a surviving unmarried partner) may by concession be allowed part or all of what you leave if the Crown is satisfied that provision is reasonable in the circumstances. But they have to apply. They are not considered automatically.

Claims under the 1975 Inheritance Act

Wills and the intestacy rules spell out who has a right to inherit. The 1975 Act allows certain people to cut across such rights and claim –

maybe more, or maybe just something.

A claim must be made (by starting court proceedings) within six months of probate or letters of administration (the equivalent of probate if there is no will). So if you think you may have a claim on the estate of someone who has died, or if you receive such a claim, see a solicitor immediately. You will need a solicitor. This is not a DIY area.

Who can claim what?

1. Surviving husbands and wives may claim reasonable financial provision (which may include additional provision) out of their partners' estates if the rules of intestacy or any will do not already make such provision for them.

2. Any of the following may claim reasonable provision for their maintenance if it has not otherwise been made:

    (a) A spouse separated under a formal Decree of Judicial Separation.

    (b) A divorced former spouse if there has been no clean break order and the spouse has not remarried.

    (c) Any child of the deceased natural or legally adopted.

    (d) Any stepchild who the deceased treated as a child of his or her family at any time.

    (e) Any other person who was being maintained in whole or in part by the deceased immediately before death. This category includes unmarried people who live together but not those who had already separated before the deceased died.

How are claims decided?

Husbands or wives who have a right to claim may hope to end up with the same sort of provision as they might have obtained after divorce, but beyond that it is impossible to lay down guidelines for these cases. The courts have to consider all the circumstances of everyone involved (including their financial circumstances); and to balance the interests of any claimant against those of the people who will otherwise inherit. So long standing unmarried partners may qualify for more than husbands or wives if the deceased ceased to live with them years ago. And children and stepchildren may qualify for more substantial provision than more distant relatives or other beneficiaries – even if those children are getting on in years and to all intents and purposes are independent.

Although (because of the time limits) these cases almost always start with a court application most of them are settled by agreement, usually on advice from skilled barristers, and do not end up in court. Legal costs almost always concentrate everyone's minds on settlement. The costs usually come out of the estate. And they may threaten all of it if a number of claimants and beneficiaries each have to be represented.

Remember these points if you are involved in any such claim – attacking or defending.

Other points to remember

1. You can easily land your intended beneficiaries with a costly law suit as your memorial if you do not provide reasonably for someone who is entitled to such provision. If you have relatives or dependants who may have a right to claim on your estate under the 1975 Inheritance Act, you should, if possible, make a will which includes reasonable provision for them. If you are in any doubt about the adequacy of what you intend ask a solicitor for advice.
2. You cannot stop anyone who has rights under the 1975 Inheritance Act from making a claim. But you may help your executors (and the courts) to resist claims of little merit if you leave a letter with your will which spells out good and compelling reasons for your will as you have chosen to make it.

Remember that if a crunch comes over your estate you will not be there to give your reasons – indeed, no one but you may ever know what they were unless you spell them out in writing in advance. But any letter written with that in mind needs careful preparation – a solicitor's advice and help is almost essential.

Appendix: Reform of the grounds for divorce

New proposals

In 1990 the Law Commission recommended the following basic changes to divorce law:

1. Once a marriage has lasted for 12 months either or both spouses should be able to start proceedings for divorce (or formal Decree of Judicial Separation) by taking to a Divorce County Court a statement (special form, of course) which says that they believe their marriage has broken down and they wish to make arrangements for the future.
2. The court should then direct how financial and any children's issues should be resolved; and the divorce itself should then be delayed to allow their resolution and scope for conciliation.
3. Neither party should be able to apply for a Decree of Divorce until all financial and children's matters are sorted out – or within 11 months of the date of the original statement if they are sorted out within that time.
4. After that period a divorce should be granted one month after either or both of the parties applies to the court stating that they believe the breakdown of their marriage is irreparable.

Progress to date

1. In 1993 the Lord Chancellor published a Green Paper seeking comment on the new proposals. Such Green Papers usually signal that new law is on its way. But although the Green Paper proposals were widely welcomed by many of those who understand how the present law works, they were strongly opposed

by others who believed that they would make divorce easier.

2. Bowing to their political pressure the Lord Chancellor returned the Green Paper proposals to the back-burner.

3. Nevertheless, the proposals may still become law some time during the 1990s. For they would solve most of the real problems in the present law:

(a) Spouses would have to sort out all their financial and children's problems before divorce instead of afterwards as now.

(b) The minimum 11-month period for doing that would allow time for reflection and conciliation which the present system does not; and it certainly would not make divorce itself easier – cases based on adultery and unreasonable behaviour under the existing law offer almost instant divorce with no time for anything (see Chapter 12, pages 80–81).

(c) Unlike the present law the proposals face up to the realities of marriage breakdown:

- A marriage has no future if either partner is absolutely determined to end it.
- If one partner is determined to end a marriage, insisting that one must prove bad conduct by the other before the marriage can be ended legally nothing is achieved except pointless additional insult and injury to all involved – including any children.

Sources of further information

The Good Retirement Guide, Rosemary Brown, 1995
How to Write a Will and Gain Probate, 5th edition, Marlene Garsia,
   1995
Letting Residential Property, Frances M Way, 1993
Living Abroad: The Daily Telegraph Guide, Michael Furnell, 1994
Living Together, Frances M Way, 1995
Splitting Up: A Legal and Financial Guide to Separation and Divorce,
   3rd edition, David Green, 1995

Index